SIX FEET
TO
Independence

Understanding Life With a Service Dog

Lauryn Walton

TitleTown Publishing, LLC
P.O. Box 12093 Green Bay, WI 54307-12093
920.737.8051 | titletownpublishing.com

Publisher: Tracy C. Ertl
Editor: Lori A. Preuss

Publisher's Cataloging-in-Publication
(Provided by Cassidy Cataloguing Services, Inc.)

Names: Walton, Lauryn, author.

Title: Six feet to independence : understanding life with a service dog / Lauryn Walton.

Description: Green Bay, WI : TitleTown Publishing, [2023]

Identifiers: ISBN: 9781955047203
                9781955047180 (eBook)

Subjects:
LCSH: Service dogs--Handbooks, manuals, etc. | Animals as aids for people with disabilities-- Handbooks, manuals, etc. | Human-animal relationships--Handbooks, manuals, etc. | BISAC: PETS / Dogs / Training & Showing.

Classification:
LCC: HV1569.6 .W35 2023 | DDC: 362.4/0483--dc23

To those who pushed me to write this--Dr. Kim, Nicole Roth, and my mum. I never thought my first book was going to be nonfiction, that's for sure. Here's to oh, so many more now that the dam has broken.

Foot One:

Laying the Groundwork

1. Are You Ready For This?

So. You've decided you want to get a service dog.

Congratulations.

Good luck.

May the odds be ever in your favor. All that stuff. A lot of people think they know what life with a service dog is like, or at least, they don't think there's much they don't know.

I think most people who think that are wrong. I think a lot of people who don't think much about service dogs would be surprised to hear how much they assume and how much of that is just plain wrong.

This book is written from first- or second-hand personal stories. This IS NOT a be-all, end-all guide, or a book in which everything applies to every situation.

We're going to take a look at just how big the difference in lifestyle between service dog handlers and non-service dog handlers is and some of what to expect if that is the adventure you choose. I'll be using my own personal story, tried and trusted information shared by reputable trainers and breeders who know their stuff and have successfully trained multiple service dogs for various handlers and their unique task needs, and handlers living the service dog life. We're real. We're raw. We're authentic. We believe you deserve nothing less.

As you will see in the following pages, the service dog journey is not an easy one. I want to help ease that difficulty as much as I can, so I have a special gift for you at www.fieldsoffavor. us/gift/. A cheat sheet summary of the ten biggest things I would've taken away from this book when I was just starting out. Click on over to get it sent directly to your email. :)

Again, I'm so proud of you for doing your research on this journey!

2. How Did We Get Here?

This is a question many ask on adventures, and I am no exception. Standing where I am now, I find myself asking this question several times. What one-off choices had to be made for me to be standing here? What would have changed if I had made one small difference in a choice? And what *on earth* makes me qualified to write this book on the service dog lifestyle? Two words: Experience. Connections.

Not just mine; oh, good heavens, not just mine. The experience and connections of people I know, those who can tell stories of other service dog lives. Those who grow and expand the worldbuilding, if you will.

Here's the thing. Once Cor and I finish training, he will be my first service dog, but I have started and restarted this journey four times.

I fight the monster called petite mal seizures. At least, that's how my monster shows itself. The actual thing I'm fighting doesn't show up in tests or anything like that as seizures.

Before you start thinking of convulsing and blue lips and not breathing, no, that's not what I have--that's my sister's monster. The one I'm dealing with... it's a bit harder to see than that. Petite mal seizures are more of a human DVD skip rather than the scariest swoon ever.

On the outside, it doesn't look like much happens. Maybe my eyes go out of focus, and my breathing changes for three seconds, but that's about it. On my side, though, it's the most inconvenient form of time travel. Me and my friends (...okay, siblings) are sitting around a table talking about our favorite... I don't know, let's say our favorite movies, and then--what feels like the next second to me--person A has gotten up to get more napkins, and we're discussing favorite ice cream flavors. As I said, the most inconvenient form of time travel. There's no warning, no sense of time passing while I'm in it; just an 'oh, poop. What'd I miss?' on the back end. To look at me at any other time, though, you wouldn't think I had anything going on save for an unreal number of allergies.

For those of you who have noticed, yes, I am actively not saying disabili**, because I'm not. I'm not "not able to do things." If you break that word down, that's what you end up with--unable. I'm not unable. Many people with these kinds of challenges aren't disabled; we are simply on a different adventure than others. And, as I am a huge story lover, I talk about it as though I were fighting a monster, demon, dragon, or something of that sort. I generally use the terms interchangeably, but I'm going to try to keep it uniform in this book by referring to it as a "monster" because that's enough of a general term that it could cover any of the other terms people may use. And, quite frankly, I want a dragon, so making it as though I'm fighting one... yeah... I'm calling it a monster. :)

Now that you know why I'm getting a service dog, I'm going to give a bit of background as to how we got here because-- like I said--I've tried to finish this journey a few times.

In order to explain the entire story, we're going to have to go back to the beginning.

Well, to be fair, my monster first showed itself on the scene about sixteen years ago. That's not the part of the story we are talking about here, though--maybe another time. So I'm starting us out roughly three years ago.

My heart has always been for rescues--giving a home and a chance to a dog who didn't have one. Saving the one who saved me. Helping other creatures who may not have the best view of themselves find the hero within them that every great story helps the characters discover.

We started discussing the idea of a service dog in March 2018. I loved the idea, not only for the freedom it would give me as I stood at eighteen, looking at the looming precipice of adulthood in front of me. As someone who can't even cross a parking lot without supervision, lest I should have a seizure in the middle of the crossing and serve as an unexpected speed bump for some poor driver who's expecting an adult to be aware of her surroundings, living on my own and driving were looking like insurmountable no-nos. Apart from that, though, it has always been my intention to get a pet dog, and if I could get a pet, put in a little bit of work to bump it up to service dog status and get tax-write-offs for its supplies as a result... well, that would be absolutely wonderful!

Nota bene: as you will find out, I had a very romantic, extremely inaccurate idea of what I was getting into.

We explored a few options and stumbled across an owner-training program. We reached out, and it virtually fell flat after the first conversation. The requirements for that program, in particular, and the lack of communication led us back to step one.

About six months later, we found Amanda Pratt at Scout's Legacy. One Saturday night, my mom shared the website with me, and we decided to send a private message. We expected to hear back sometime next week. When the message was answered within the hour, our hope soared again! We set up a phone call to ask questions and, about a week later, went on an outing to see what a group training session looked like, to meet Amanda, and to get our first introduction into the service dog world. We knew this would be our pack. I just needed to start saving and preparing. So I started a blog! (Check it out at www.fieldsoffavor.us)

About a year after we decided to start exploring the options the service dog world held, six months after meeting Amanda and starting to save money for the training--surely just a few hundred dollars, right?--someone on our neighborhood Facebook page put out that they were looking to re-home their dog; was anyone looking for one?

What are the odds? What could go wrong from here, right?
Ha.
Haha.
Muahahahaha...!
Yeah, my hopeful former self... couldn't be more wrong.
See, we met the dog and reached out to our trainer, raving. We found a dog--lab and Aussie mix--that we thought would be *perfect*. Could we meet up soon and have her temperament test him?

Of course! There was a group outing coming up, and if we brought him, she'd run him through the test before they got going.

We had him over for a day and a night before the meeting. Our spoken thought was that this was to get to the group outing easier and quicker. The real hope was that, at this time, we'd warm up to each other--because *clearly,* that'd clearly be a part of the test. Note to former self: think again.

I had planned on letting him sleep in my bed with me, but after a surprise introduction to humping, I decided I wasn't quite ready for that yet. I closed my door, and he spent the night with his back pressed up against it, trying to get as close to me as he could.

As it turned out, getting along well wasn't part of the test at all. Go figure.

We brought Ozzy to the training and--now that I know Amanda's facial expressions so much better--I can tell you that her face went from, "hi! so good to see y'all again!" to "oh, good *heavens*, what kind of a mess have they brought me?" And that language is on the milder side.
What she said was more along the lines of, 'well... as a business woman, I could tell you you can try training with him, but when (and, nonverbally, if) he makes it through, you're going to have to start training the next one pretty much immediately due to his age.' She also pointed out that he was a hound (not a lab/Aussie mix--which, now that I know more, I can tell you would be a mix she wouldn't have advised us as beginners to start with, either.)

And, because he had been allowed to let his nose lead him for this long, going out into public would likely be *very hard* for most of the training.

In other words: please don't make any of us deal with this. We didn't.

The next option came along on the exact day I zonked out in the car from physical exertion on our way to return Ozzy to his pet home and wish his owner good luck finding him a forever family.

A friend of a friend had been fostering a shelter dog. The dog had had puppies, and would we be interested in seeing if they would be able to be a service dog?

Oh, Amanda...! Could you temperament test more puppies for us?

Well, out of the litter of seven pups, one of them passed. And, y'all, he was *SO cute*! Paws too big for his body, all tan and black and white splotches, all panty grins. And he passed! All I had to do was adopt him, and he'd be mine!

Y'all, the only love-at-first-sight situation I've had in my life led to a ten-year (extremely unhealthy) as-far-as-I-know-unrequited crush in grade school and this? This left that in the *dust*. I was head over heels in love with this puppy. I had a name and everything already--Teddy. It meant 'precious gift,' and he just *looked* like the cuddliest little teddy bear to ever grace the earth.

...you see where this is going, right?

But he passed! He was mine! Mine, mine, mine!

...and then we went to the shelter to adopt him.

Let me take a minute here and explain something. I need a mobility dog, not just a seizure response dog.

In the opinion of many trainers, for the safety of the dog and handler, and just out of decency for the dog, it's important to let the dog (especially a mobility service dog) mature unaltered, so they can not only learn to control their... *ahem*... baser urges, but also to let their hormones do what they need to do to help them grow up the right way--barring against joint dysplasia in the future as best as we can--by letting the joints grow to match the sockets in full.

The state of Texas has an equally understandable but completely opposite view on it--they can't let dogs be adopted without being altered since there are already too many homeless dogs--we don't need to condone dogs' baser urges producing more.

These two arguments both make sense, and I am not speaking against either.

However, you can't side with both, can you?

We tried to come to a compromise. The young man we were talking to, though, was an assistant manager. He had no power to really change anything. We understood the dilemma he was in and asked who we needed to talk to to get an answer about it.

Armed with a name and a number on a piece of paper and the promise she'd be in the next day, we reached out to Amanda--this is what was going on. Did she see any chances for compromise? Anyway through this? Any words we should use or stay away from to get the desired results?

Her response surprised us and was a bit disappointing at the moment: "well... I have another dog that was just offered up for our program. Would you be interested in him?"

The transfer of attention was so sudden in our minds that we nearly experienced whiplash.

He was a rescue, found abandoned by the side of the road. The lady who found him tried to find his people for about a month. She had had a service dog before, knew the temperament, knew what was needed, and this boy stood out to her as perfect for the job. He was very aware of her moods and what was going on beneath the surface; he'd offer extra snuggles just when she needed it, and--as unreliable as looking at a puppy is for determining the long-term temperament of a dog, he seemed perfect. He looked like he had been groomed recently, but no one had lost a dog. She knew Amanda from working within the dog world, so she called her and offered him up (for free) to anyone in the program if he passed the temperament test, which he did--he wasn't easily spooked, was eager to learn, didn't shy away from new or strange places, loved people, and all the other things that a temperament test reveals in a dog.

My heart sank. But I needed closure with Teddy before we moved forward with another dog--if I could've done something and simply given up too early, I'd never forgive myself.

The next day we went to the Humane Society location that he would be adopted through, hoping those who knew him and his mother could maybe lobby in our favor rather than the bigger, more central, less personal (in regards to him) location; hoping that they'd have the authority to address the problem we were having.

We had some ideas we thought were good and some we'll admit may have been a stretch. Would it change things if we got a letter from our trainer explaining why this was a need? What if we signed something that said we wouldn't let him... well, we weren't breeding him and that we'd be responsible for any (nonexistent) puppies that may result. Maybe we could come up with some sort of partnership between the Humane Society and our training program--Scout's Legacy--so that the only unaltered puppies they were releasing would be going to train as service dogs, and those that didn't make it would be trained by those who have an interest in seeing them succeed--possibly helping them go to homes that wouldn't go looking for untrained dogs with unknown backgrounds or levels of behavior. That could benefit both organizations to the point that we could surely work something out, right...?

No. The best the lady (who was extremely understanding and nice and all the things) said they could allow us was six months. That way, any females they adopted out wouldn't hit a cycle where things could happen. And by things, I mean puppies.

We couldn't alter Teddy until he was two years old, though, so six months wasn't going to cut it.

This dog that had passed the temperament test--that I had fallen in love with and already considered mine... I wasn't going to be able to get him.

After acknowledging and mourning the loss of Teddy, whom I had let myself hope for and dream about--we moved forward with the other dog--he was a rescue, too, so of course, I wanted to give him a good home. Of course, I wanted to save him. Of course, I wanted to let myself dream of each of us giving the other the love and support we each needed from a very specific source that others couldn't fill. But I was scared, you guys. So, so scared.

I had held myself away from Ozzy because, I think, right when I saw him pulling his owner around on their "walk," I knew he wasn't going to pass. But I had let myself get close to the idea of Teddy.

But I had another chance, and I couldn't punish this dog for my heartbreak with Teddy.

I named him Yahaloam--Hebrew for precious stone, because we were both diamonds in the rough, and everyone says a diamond is a girl's best friend, right?

Y'all, he was so *sweet*. I let myself hope again. I let myself fall head over heels for this puppy. Again.

Love does strange things, doesn't it? Even after the pain and difficulty of Ozzy and Teddy, I let myself hope. I let myself love. I gave this creature my heart and trusted him with my life. Even though I'd been burned before, I let myself hope and love and fall again simply because this goober gave me his panty, doggy smile.

He was a ball of teeth and energy, and I loved him. I was his third home in a month to six weeks; he was my third try at this. The third time was a charm; he was mine, and I was his, and I was sure we were going to blast through the training because I had plans for my life, and he was so excited and loving. Even when his teeth were sharp and made me bleed because they slipped on the antler, he was chewing that I had somehow wound up holding.

Beyond the first meeting, the first training--where he barked at the other dogs the entire time (*facepalm*). We braved puppyhood together, including the purgatory of his teething stage. Y'all, I had to wear long jeans and cowboy boots the entire time we were both awake for about two weeks, and that was after I was about ready to cry from him getting my calves. He would grab the bottom of my jeans with the power of his lab's jaws and hold on with the tenacity we now realize he got from a German shepherd parent (*grimace*). He would grab on, hold on, and *shake*. Now, I may not weigh much--one hundred thirty-some last measurements--but I'd put my weight on that leg, and he would *still* move it. Y'all, forget anything you may have heard of in stories. That is the ultimate power.

He didn't seem to nap. At. All. Looking back on it, that wasn't healthy for either of us, but I didn't see his signs that he was over-tired.

Through it all--through times I just wanted to cry from frustration (and the little ankle-biter biting my ankles), through times when I was only able to stay with it because, on Thursdays, my family would take him for a few hours so we could get a break from each other (and yet he'd still camp out right outside my bedroom door. No one can give a guilt trip like a puppy). Through times I just had to call Amanda and go, "AHHHHHHH! WHY IS HE LIKE THIS?" just to hear her smile and assure me that it was normal--he's a puppy; they're jerks. Through it all, I loved him. Even now, I still love him. My heart has never been happier than when I can dog sit for him and see him and Cor play together.

...spoilers.

We got Yahaloam--we started calling him Yaha because Yahaloam is... well, a bit long--in March. We zoomed through training lessons and skills. We shared morning walks, went on 'ventures' (outings) nearly everywhere together, and became best buddies. We were making such progress I thought for sure he'd be the dog to finish a two-year program in one!

At the end of July, it all came crashing down around my ears.

He had hit a fear stage and wasn't taking it well. In a fear stage, as I'll go into more later, the dog starts to get a healthy fear of the world around them--realizing their mortality and that not everything revolves around them. This can often bring out hidden red flags that a puppy didn't think to act on. As Yaha was a rescue and hadn't had the best beginning in life, it hit him hard, and he started behaving almost as if he were having a delayed reaction to his first few months. He spooked far easier and was less inclined to bounce back quickly, was on edge, and worried about new places and around lots of people (read: 5+). He still loved people--once he knew they weren't going to hurt his person, which was normally after a few moments of barking when on walks. Trust issues started coming up--him being less ready to just accept people and dogs and almost more of a "you'll have to prove you're not going to hurt my girl or me." He had always been uneasy around other dogs, and--when we'd cross paths on the walks--would bark and lunge at them while I hauled on the leash to keep him from running over until someone rounded a corner, he couldn't see them anymore, and he judged us safe once more. In Amanda's words, "he had too much confidence" in himself and his duty to protect me. As he grew into himself, that's the job he took as assigned to him—protector and defender. Not so much the helper and partner I needed him to be.

At Amanda's suggestion, we decided to try a "puppy vacation" and a bit of a break for two to three weeks. I had already had a trip to visit family planned. Convenient. So we stopped going out as much. We backed off a bit with the training.

The weeks passed; I went away. He learned how to not need to be constantly moving and doing--one of the hardest lessons to teach him to date. So we continued for another month and a half, getting through yet more lessons. He was doing so well, and I was sure he'd turned a corner. That we'd fixed it and were back to the speedy, 'blasting through' team we had been.

So when I heard Amanda's fateful "we need to consider the chance we'll need to wash him," it felt like I'd failed him. Like

I should have done more. Could've done better. Had failed the boy who had only ever given me love. My scalp did the turn-cold-and-tingle thing that has always signaled panic. I'd only had him for four months. But those four months felt so much longer and were so full of love and work and pain and struggling through it together--or, what I thought was together, at least. Yaha was supposed to be the one. He'd been doing so well--flying through so fast, blowing past others who'd been in the program months longer than us (and maybe cultivating a bit of unhealthy competition in his handler). The third time was supposed to be the charm, so how could this be something we were even considering?

And yet... I saw it. I saw it in the way he watched everything but me when we were in public. I saw it in the way he'd whine under my chair at the doctor's office. I saw it in the way he'd bark at any dog we walked past as though they were going to attack me. He loved me. He wanted to please me. He wanted the treats. But he didn't like--and was dreading--the job every time we went out. Not a position that's good for a service dog to be in. So we stopped going out as much. We backed off a bit with the training.

Dogs go through puppyhood in a way that sort of resembles a wave pool. There are various 'stages,' or waves, that will crash over your head as you bob up and down. There are what are called "fear stages," "adolescent stages," and another stage that doesn't necessarily have an official name because everyone's just grateful to get there and be able to relax--"normal stage," for lack of a better term.

In the adolescent stage, the dog tests boundaries and rules and limits, seeing what they can get away with and trying to make the world "theirs."

In the fear stage, it's like they've never been in this world before--things that were no problem previously are suddenly the scariest things on earth, and they can't handle it. (We'll go deeper into those a bit later.)

Yaha was caught in a fear stage with no idea what to do with these new "big boy" feelings. Going out on "ventures" and outings was only making those feelings worse and more acute. Instead of letting him be confident in what he knew, I was forcing him into a strange and unknown world--something he didn't know how to handle, on top of some other problems.

Let me pause quickly and explain. When we were first considering getting into the service dog world, my youngest sister, Josie, campaigned hard for German shepherds for a couple of reasons; the largest of them? Boys.

Amanda nipped that one in the bud right away. Why? Because German shepherds were bred to be herding dogs. They were bred to protect and guard. Me and my sister, Marina, are battling the monsters of seizures, joint hyper-elasticity, and other various autoimmune stuff. In this situation, we sometimes need help from others. However, the dog's natural tendency would be to guard us--to put itself between its person and whoever was coming, presumably (to the dog) to hurt us--and warn the other off. They would be trying to protect us, but the way they'd naturally try to protect us would actually be doing the opposite. Because if the service dog wasn't letting those who could help get close, the service dog would be actively doing the opposite of what it should be.

That's where Yaha was running into trouble. He became so protective that it was becoming distracting and overwhelming to him. That caused frustration in both of us.

My frustration was because I was trusting him with my well-being, and he wasn't getting it. That led to problems because Yaha was supposed to help fight the monsters, thus helping with the anxiety coming from said monsters. Instead, he was causing more anxiety by being another thing to try to control, keep track of, and handle.

This situation was causing frustration in him because he was *trying*, and why couldn't his human *see* that? He was doing what his human wanted; why wasn't that enough for her?

Y'all, that's not a good position for a service dog or handler to be in. So when, in September, Amanda confirmed that, yeah, he was done, and I handed in the vest... as heartbreaking as it was, it was almost a relief for the both of us. I was able to take a deep breath and acknowledge that love doesn't equal compatibility. I was able to look Amanda in the eyes with Yaha in my arms and finally admit that the goal was a fully-trained service dog, even if it wasn't a rescue. I couldn't go through this again. This couldn't be a trial-and-error way of learning.

The hardest part was, Yaha had become so protective that he wouldn't *let* another dog work with me while he was still living in the house. We had no choice but to re-home him.

When I was able to form words, they were, "Please find me a breed, and find me a breeder. But can I please help rehome him? I can't move on without closure. Without *knowing* he's in a good place. Without *knowing* that *he* knows I'm not abandoning him. That I'm not number three, but that I'm still trying to help him."

Amanda agreed--something I will be grateful for until my dying breath.

So we started looking. From September through November, Yaha lived with us as a retired pet as I reached out to breeders Amanda had sent me, researched and asked questions, and tried to estimate birth days and pick-up days while getting no after no about Yaha's new home. He was such a good boy. Maybe not the best with other dogs--of which half the people in the neighborhood seemed to have, and the other half weren't looking for. He was a bit big for the families of the kids I did childcare for at church (2-3 year-olds), but he was *such* a good boy that only wanted to make his people happy. How was he having this much trouble finding a home? As painful as it was to meet with people over and over again, always deciding that--for one reason or another--it wasn't a good fit, I am grateful I was able to have a hand in it.

I was in the middle of a gut-wrenching discussion with my mom about reaching out to Amanda to help us find Yaha's new home, a move I knew meant I would possibly not hear of nor see him again. I was about to admit we'd tried our best, but maybe we just didn't know his forever home when a Facebook message came through on my phone.

I asked my mom if she knew the name of the person who had sent the message; it was a family we knew of from church. They were friends of friends, and we'd seen them around on Sunday mornings and Wednesday evenings but didn't know them very well.

"I can't believe I'm doing this," the message read. "Is Yaha still looking for a home?"

They were still dealing with emotions from losing a dog the month before (also a black lab) and weren't sure whether they were ready for another dog so soon.

Yes, he was. After a bit of a discussion, it was suggested that they come over and meet him the next night while their girls were at youth group and I was working childcare.

I didn't see the magic moment, but I've heard it raved about on both sides. Something we had worked with Yaha on (and worked and worked and worked) was settling down--not always needing to be *doing* something. And he was starting to get it. Or maybe, that, too, was wishful thinking.

But, apparently, the husband only needed to tell Yaha "down" once after getting him all excited and playing quite enthusiastically with him. And Yaha did it without argument, happy to just lie down beside him! Apparently, by the end of the night, everyone was in love.

But no one wanted to make this decision on emotion (and, remember, I wasn't even there), so we all decided to give it a day to think before making any kind of decision.

About twenty-one hours later, Mom and I were talking about the possibility of reaching out to Amanda because we hadn't heard and wanted to be prepared if this one were to fall through when the text came (again):

"We want him. When would be best for us to pick him up?" This was a Thursday night, and we started to talk about the weekend. Gradually, it came out that something a bit... sooner... might be better.

How much sooner?

Well, not three hours later, I, too, had fallen in love with this family for Yaha, and we were waving goodbye as Yaha trotted off beside his new people to their car.

Y'all, that moment. I cannot think of a better picture of bittersweet unless it was about three months later--the week before we got Cor--when we next saw Yaha and visited his family.

We all came in and said hi. Yaha was doing SO much better meeting new people than he ever did when he was with us when he did the *clearest* double-take and jumped up on me. Y'all, the wicked witch of the west would've melted under all the kisses he gave me.

It was so clear he was so happy with his new family. He is going through "pet training" as a walking/running companion and is loving his new family. And! I'm their on-call dogsitter. :)

Now, back it up a few months, back to when we were looking for a new puppy. We had decided on a poodle pretty quickly for reasons I'll explain later. We asked our trainer if she had any responsible standard poodle breeders she'd recommend, and she gave us a bit of a list that we started looking into.

Y'all, if you thought the story was a bit wild up until now, just wait.

We visited the website of one of the breeders and found that one of their females was expecting (!!!). There was an active waiting list that we could request to get on. The only problem with that is one with which I refer you back to Teddy. Most of the puppies in a litter won't pass the temperament test. Teddy was the only one in his litter, and normally the magic number is about two when any given litter will have about five to seven puppies. This isn't the exact number for all litter, just an average. We reached out to see if they had any special situations for puppies that people were looking to adopt as service dogs.

Well... they *do*... but the mama had absorbed her puppies, meaning she was no longer pregnant, and that waiting list was null. Now, full disclosure, here--I had no idea that could happen, but apparently, it had happened with this female before, sooo....

Back to square one.

We looked into the other breeders Amanda had sent us information on.

Mom fell in love with one as soon as she read the first words of their home page: *It all started at a dog park over a beer... Yes, in Austin, Texas, we are lucky enough to have a dog park that serves beer.*

As I said, Mom fell in love instantly and said we had to at least reach out to them. My mom was raised in Wisconsin and always had a bit of a stereotype around poodles and how fancy they can be. To be fair, so did I. For the most part. Beer seemed to help normalize the poodle idea for her. I was a bit more hesitant. (A mom can absorb her babies?!? Am I signing up for just as much emotional pain, difficulty, and waiting as *training* the dog by looking to *get* a dog?)

After a loving, verbal kick in the pants (as I need every once in a while), I started to research. I started to dig in a bit and look at this breeder to see what I could find. It all lined up, and I started to feel a bit better about trying again (and saving up to do so). We reached out and found out that they had a female that was due to go into heat soon, and they were putting together a wait list for said puppies. They directed me to the contract of 'I will take care of the puppy in X way, and will not do Y. I will let you know if I do Q, and will keep you up to date with pictures and info'. And, no, it wasn't a two-sentence thing. Try more like four pages. Oddly enough, this made me much more comfortable with these people because they take their puppies' safety and home life seriously. I'll go into breeder red and green flags more a bit later, but, for now, the large part is that responsible or "good" breeders care more about the puppies' futures and health than the money they can make on said puppies--such breeders are out there, you just have to look.

I want to camp here for a moment and go into a few other above-and-beyond things I found in researching FIGZ Poodles because we could not have asked for a better breeder for Cor.

FIGZ breeds their dogs for the service dog temperament, specifically. This means that quality comes before aesthetics and pretty coats. Now, if you look at their website (www.figzservicedogs.com, in case anyone is wondering) and social media pages, you will see that their dogs' appearances in no way suffer from this focus. I mean, look at the picture on the back cover and tell me that it is not the most photogenic poodle you've ever seen. But, because of this focus, not only do their breeding dogs have show titles before and after their names, but the vast majority are also either service dogs or service dogs in training. Cor is a third-generation service dog, in fact.

More than looking for the best lines to breed service dogs, they also stand by their dogs. That sounds simple and like it'd be an obvious necessity for responsible breeders--and it is--but FIGZ takes it above and beyond expectation. Not only do they breed for service dog temperament, but they also train service dogs themselves--mostly their own puppies. They see these dogs all the way through. From how their parents' and grandparents' health is, through conception and training, and are always on call for those who get their dogs. I will share a story later about when this particular aspect of "always on call" may very well have saved Cor's life.

Okay. One contract and a couple of thousand dollars in an envelope later, we were just waiting on the female to go into heat.

It shouldn't take long, right? I mean, I cycle every month--how long can it be between a dog's "in heat" times?

Yeah... so apparently, dogs only go into heat every six months.

Lucky dogs.

Three months later, we were still waiting, wishing Newt a happy New Year, a happy Valentine's *cough, cough*, hoping we wouldn't get to a happy Mother's Day, *ahem* and all the things-- may she start feeling the love! (!!!)

Now, for any of you who have been keeping up with the math, that likely doesn't make sense, right? I mean, three months later, it was a week before we got Cor, and we were visiting Yaha, so how could we still be waiting for the female to go into heat? That's not how having babies works. Granted, a dog's incubation doesn't take as long as a human's, but it's still not that short.

That's where things start to get a bit... wild.

One Friday late afternoon, I had been near tears--just brought down and dragged through the mud. I was happy Yaha had a home, and I was glad I was able to get another dog, but they'd said she'd go into heat soon. What was going on? Was this some sort of sign that this just wasn't the road I was supposed to be on? Nothing was happening, and it felt like I just kept getting dragged back to square one. I asked my parents if we could just go wander around the local pet store. I just needed to feel like this could happen again--that I wasn't fighting a losing battle, stubbornly not listening to all the signs and warnings. Remember, this wasn't the selfish road.

My dad, sisters and I drove to the pet store not five minutes down the road. (Oh, I think I forgot to mention--those petite mal seizures? Yeah, because of those, I can't drive. I'm 21 and still have a chauffeur-Mom/Dad.) On our way, we listened to some audiobook or other. I honestly can't remember because the text I got kind of froze everything around me. It was from the breeders.

So, still waiting on [the female] to go into heat. However, one of our males sired a litter with [another female] of Pure Southern Poodles. [As per the arrangement we made with them], we get one of the puppies. We were going to train him as a service dog before we remembered you had said you were looking for a male. Would you be interested in him?

Y'all, I can't remember how many times I had to reread that message. I legitimately believe I fell into shock.

After sitting on it so as to not make this decision out of sheer emotion, I started running through my budget to see if it could take it to start right now as opposed to receiving, at the very least, eight weeks' notice. It could.

Oh, glory.

What about coming up dogsitting and trips?

They could be arranged to accommodate a puppy or, at that time, an adolescent dog.

Oh, heavens.

What about work and plans?

Yes. We could make it work.

Oh, gosh. I need to sit down.

A crate. A puppy was going to need a different size than a seventy-pound dog (Yaha got BIG, y'all).

A friend of ours was able to let us borrow theirs.

Toys...?

We can go to the store before getting him.

...

Food?

Figured out.

I think I'm getting dizzy. But... yeah. I... I'd love to take him. Can we have a call to chat? That night, with my feet far more attuned to the speed of the earth's spinning, we had a call with the breeders to see what would need to happen for this to move forward.

After a few more questions and answers were thrown around and everything was smoothed out--and I was starting to grasp that this actually was happening, we all agreed this was looking great and ready to roll.

This is another time FIGZ showed just how much of a labor of love this work is for them. Because he had been with his mother's people for his entire seven-week life, they wanted to keep him for a week-long puppy boot camp with April--the

Certified Canine Training and Behavior Specialist they have on staff (!!!) so they could get a feel for him. That way, should I have questions or concerns about him in the future, they could answer them because they knew him. Also, because the amount I paid for him covered post-natal training in service dog work, they wanted to double-check that he was up to their standards and that I was getting my money's worth. Could I sleep with a towel or shirt for a few days, then drop that and a few cotton swabs of during-the-seizure saliva off so they could start scent training with him?

Of course. When and where?

At the end of that puppy boot camp week, they had a dog show on the eighth (of March. In 2020) where we could meet to hand him off. (Maybe not so coincidentally, my trainer was also at that same dog show.) Does that work for you as a place to meet?

...Yeah, yeah, of course, it does.

Cor is a third-generation service dog with titles behind Mom and Dad's names, as well as through his bloodlines. I could tell the difference as soon as he got home--as soon as he was placed in my arms by the breeders, more accurately.

If he was tired, he'd plop down and sleep anywhere. Contrast that with Yaha, who I needed to put in the crate to get him to believe he could rest right now. He is able to sit and watch the world go by. Contrast that with Ozzy, who we played fetch with for hours on his first day with us. He listens (most of the time) to what I ask him to do. Contrast that with the pet dog we had before we moved to Texas, who had the mental and physical power and wherewithal to just ignore us should we ask her to do anything she didn't want to.

Clearly, this would be a fast sprint to the finish line ending with a slide to shame any professional baseball player, right?

Of course, eight days after getting him, we were all relegated to quarantine, so Cor and I became part of the puppy generation that my trainer likes to call "pandemic puppies." I'll go into why that makes a difference in the growth of a puppy mentally later.

May I also refer you back to the breed of 'poodle,' which did not get stereotypes for no reason. He's a stubborn little sucker that will get jealous of other dogs at the drop of a hat. He's a picky eater that will simply not eat breakfast some days in favor of waiting it out for his raw meat blend for dinner. And he has a different approach toward fear stages.

The way my trainer puts it, Yaha was too confident, while Cor was not confident enough. His confidence stems from me and my presence, which is all well and good until it isn't. We were at a training (yesterday, as I write this) when that started to show signs of being problematic. I had him in down-stay, and other handlers were helping the group practice for distractions the dogs will experience that most (me, before I entered the program, included) wouldn't think to expect.

This was an exercise we'd practiced before. Maybe not for a little while, but he'd never had a big problem with it. It was a bit weird, but he'd get to the "whatever, humans are just weird" point rather quickly. Last night, though? He saw the person coming, broke his stay, trotted over, and leaned against my legs to hide.

Normally, this kind of behavior is classified as cute, and I get it--there's nothing quite like the feeling when a dog chooses you to trust to the point of finding comfort from you. When that dog is in training to be a service dog, though, this kind of behavior can get dangerous fast. I need to be able to depend on him to know what he needs to do and not shy away from doing so. If the dog can't do what it needs to do, there's no more point in bringing them out in public than there is in bringing a pet to a store simply because you want to.

Amanda stepped in. She told me to walk out of sight, and she worked Cor for the rest of the exercise.

Having gone through a wash with Yaha, my brain started connecting phrases, thoughts, and sights that didn't need to be. I started filling in the next six months as I stood there, and Amanda went to the next exercise--the dogs working with other people.

I freaked out--silently so as not to interrupt the group. If I couldn't get Cor to do the thing, what made me think I could get another dog that I knew nothing about (I missed his name and sex for the first half of the exercise) to do it? If Cor wouldn't do the thing with me, what made us think he would do it with another person? It didn't help that the dog I was paired with decided to be a stinker while he was working with me.

We were, again, working in down-stays, and he wouldn't even listen to me when I told him to lie down. He knew how clearly--I'd seen his person doing tasks far ahead of "down" earlier in training--he just wasn't listening to me.

Yaha washed, Cor was spooking for some reason, and this other dog that didn't even know me apparently knew I wasn't the one in charge. The only common denominator was me; I had to be the reason these dogs were failing--it was my fault, and I was ruining perfectly good dogs. I was hurting their chances of being all that they could be, and I shouldn't have started doing this in the first place. I was hurting the dogs and the people they could've helped, and, and, and...

As I said, I started to freak out.

I saw Mom and Amanda talking with solemn faces and quiet voices several yards away as people continued what we were doing--a mix of recall ("come!") and leave it. As I said, my mind was filling in the conversation as I stood there, watching them, recalling the struggle and panic of the last few months with Yaha. My mind kept portraying the next six months with Cor the same way and needing to start over again, going through puppyhood for a third time while dealing with yet another bout of heartbreak in losing a dog.

A friend of mine was working with Cor. She's had a handful of service dogs already and is one of the trainers in the organization. After the training, I couldn't get over to her fast enough, trying to figure out her thoughts on this. We ended up as the last ones still in the store. She, Mom, and Amanda spent several minutes explaining that this wasn't like Yaha--we weren't talking about a possible wash, but that this is something that needed to be addressed--he needs to be able to build confidence in himself apart from me. In other words, he needs to be worked by other people.

Okay... fine. That's all well and good, but I'm going back up to Wisconsin for a handful of reasons in a few days. How are we going to fit that in before I go?

...we're not. Cor is going to stay down here for at least the first part and work with my family as well as have a handful of daily training sessions with various trainers--they will take him for a few hours and work him in public and at their home.

I will mention "emergency funds" later as something you need to prepare for--this falls into that category. I hadn't planned for this, I hadn't known to prepare for it, but I need the money for it, and I need it now. The good news is that I had approached paychecks and earnings with the foresight (thanks to Amanda's and my parents' advice) to start a bit of a fall-back fund. I was able to cover it, thanks to their counsel. Consider *this* an illustration as to why you need this sort of fund. (I'm just grateful it wasn't a five thousand dollar emergency vet bill--they exist.)

When I heard this--that Cor was staying home--I started to panic again. I was going up to Wisconsin and leaving my dog down here?? Like, what happened with Yaha at the beginning of the end?? I wouldn't have been surprised if my face had lost all color. I hadn't seen it coming with Yaha; did I not see it coming with Cor? Was he going to wash, too?

Again, the reassurances came that this wasn't like Yaha; they would tell me if it was a concern. I knew they would-- they had with Yaha. Neither of the trainers I was talking to was concerned about this, and, according to them, every handler worried about this. Every owner-trainer had this fear at the back of their mind. Every person was aware of the possibility and was just as scared as I was. This was normal.

I breathed again.

I trust Amanda.

I trust Marleigh (the other trainer).

They have been through this so many times. They know what to look for and what they're looking at. They're not as emotionally or financially invested, and so, can look at it more analytically and rationally. I trust them. They know what they're doing. Still, I'd been burned once, and I was terrified of a repeat. Slowly, though, I started to calm down.

We must've stood there for close to half an hour after the training as I was trying to calm down and look at this rationally. Whether we fully got there or not, I don't know. I'm still trying to look at this rationally, and I see the reason we need to go forward like this, but that doesn't mean I'm not still trying to keep myself from believing the lies that it's me; I'm the reason these dogs aren't doing well. It doesn't mean I'm not terrified that I'll come back to the news that he hasn't come through it or that my being gone had made what he's going through worse, that I abandoned him when he needed me most. It doesn't mean I'm not terrified to put twelve hundred miles between my puppy and me because I am. I trust my trainers with all my heart, but I'm still terrified.

And they say that, too, is normal. So here's hoping.

Also contributing to this book with their [extensive] knowledge are:

-- Amanda Pratt--Owner and operator of Scouts Legacy Service Dogs (www,scoutslegacy.com), service dog trainer, dog breeder, and shower.

-- Kerry, Tanya, owner of FIGZ Service Dogs (www.figzservicedogs.com) and service dog trainers, dog breeders, and showers. Additionally,

Kerry is a registered respiratory therapist
Tanya is also a real estate broker, instructor, TRLP, TLRP, TLRS, and GRI.

-- Marleigh: handler of Kintsugi--[Kint]sugi is a standard poodle fully trained as a mobility, medical assistance, and psychiatric dog. Marleigh is one of Cor's day trainers, and he and I are lucky to call them both "friends."

    -- Rose family: handler of McGregor--McGregor is a pit bull mix training to be a psychiatric and mobility service dog for Abel Rose. The Rose family is the owner training McGregor.

    -- Leonard Duncan: handler of JoJo--JoJo is a standard poodle training to be a psychiatric and mobility service dog. JoJo was part of Scout's Legacy's puppy raiser program after which Leonard is now owner-training.

    -- Lauren Girsh: handler of Juno--Juno is a heeler/husky mix training to be an allergen alert, medical alert, and psychiatric dog. Lauren is owner-training Juno.

    -- Kelsey: handler of Paxton Grace--Paxton is a labrador training to be a psychiatric dog with an acute focus on anxiety response. Kelsey and Paxton are owner training.

    -- Sam: handler of Clover--Clover is a pit bull mix training to be a medical response and psychiatric dog. Sam and Clover are owner training.

    -- Janet: handler of Valor--Valor is a redbone coonhound mix training to be a hearing alert, light mobility/guiding, and psychiatric dog. Janet and Valor are owner training.

    -- River: handler of Peach--Peach is a labrador, mastiff, and rottweiler mix fully trained for mobility, psychiatric, and medical alert. River and Peach owner trained.

    -- Kaleb Kelly: handler of Roo--Roo is an American pit bull terrier/Staffordshire terrier mix training to be a psychiatric dog. Kaleb and Roo are owner-training.

    *Thank you for answering my numerous questions! Some comments may have been edited for space and context.

    Let's start with two things, if you get nothing else out of this book, I hope these settle in your mind like dried poop on your dog's rear.

    1.)   Our dogs are not perfectly behaved; they're dogs, not robots.

    2.)   Always talk to your trainer; it'll nip mistakes in the bud and save you more pain than you can imagine.

I want you to take that mindset with you into the rest of the book--always, ALWAYS, ALWAYS, ALWAYS, ALWAYS talk to your trainer. Ask questions. They are as close as you'll get to guaranteed success. Your trainer would far rather be asked more questions than you think they would than have you assume you know the answer.

I also hope you remember number one; if you don't, you'll learn it firsthand, and that's far more painful than remembering and just having grace from the beginning.

Question: What specifically would you, as a service dog trainer--as well as a handler--want me to make sure I convey and/or talk about directly?

From FIGZ: *First and foremost, service dogs are working dogs with a job to perform. It is imperative to teach the handler and the public that service dogs are not to be distracted when working. While not required to wear a vest, we recommend all service dogs wear a vest to help inform the public of their status. Service dogs are a medical device--an extension of the disabled person--that CANNOT be denied access! ADA has specific rules on dealing with service dogs in public and housing situations. A handler needs to know these laws and be able to defend their dog's presence at any given time. Service dogs are different from therapy dogs and emotional support animals. Therapy dogs and emotional support animals DO NOT have the same rights as service dogs.*

From Amanda: *I really wish people would look at their lifestyle before they would consider a service dog. A service dog is not meant to be an easy outlet. It is a hard way of helping with your disability. And for some, it is worth it. But for others, their lifestyle is not conducive to actually having a service dog, and I wish--I wish--people would sit there and consider that first before they try and get one. Many end up with pets because they realize quickly that this is way more work than they expected. And it is way harder to live with a service dog in the public eye than if they were just using a different device. For instance, those who use a cane could use a service dog, but a service dog is going to provide more attention than a cane would, and some people aren't able to live with the social distraction of everyday people asking questions and talking to them and the everyday interactions that come with a service dog.*

Question: What do you wish you could tell every person considering this life?

It's HARD. --Rose family

Service dogs aren't a magical cure-all like the media often makes them out to be - in fact, there's a lot of stress that comes with having and raising a service dog. However, even the most stressful parts of your journey with a service dog help improve your quality of life. --Leonard Duncan

The work and effort you put into the relationship with your dog are what you will get in return. --Lauren Girsh

It's not easy--by far--but it's rewarding; you not only have a partner and best friend but your lifeline. --Kelsey

Even if you've had a dog before, during your childhood (which I have not), this is completely different. Having a service dog, in my experience, is like having a toddler that needs to learn how to navigate its environment and how to think for itself; but also learn several tasks to help you when you cannot help yourself. --Sam

Every part of every day is a learning opportunity, either for you, for them, or for you both. --Anonymous

It isn't as easy or fun as it looks. I get comments all the time about how people wish they could bring their dogs everywhere with them. I've had many close calls regarding safety and other dogs in public due to the ignorance of businesses. The public will treat you like you are a circus act. If you can't overlook people pointing you out all the time, I definitely wouldn't recommend a service dog. --Janet

Do not do it unless it's completely necessary. I cannot even get a job because of my service dog being around me. They are a lot of work and a hassle to have around, even while I love them and will continue having them to help me. Think before jumping head-first into it. --River

[Note: it is illegal to refuse employment to someone just because they have a service dog--that doesn't mean it isn't done. It can be hard to pinpoint that is why you're being refused unless the employer says it point-blank, which most won't.]

It is a long road to train your own service dog, but at the end of the day, your dog becomes the most important aspect of your life. --Kaleb Kelly

It isn't easy, and it isn't right for everyone or every disability, but for me, it is absolutely the right fit, and I wouldn't change it. People with anxiety also need to be prepared that the amount of attention and interaction they get from having a service dog might make their anxiety worse to the point that having the dog isn't worth it. Personally, it was hard at first, but I got used to it, and now, most days, I don't really think about it. I have known people that the dog hurt more than helped because of the level of attention and confrontation it brought, though. --Marleigh

BE STEADFAST. Like raising children, service dogs have an endless need. Tiring and sleepless days and nights. Many hours of frustration and wanting to bang your head against the wall. The feelings of failure and the lack of respect. Exhaustion to the brink of uncontrollable crying. Yet, pure enlightenment and the resounding sense of freedom! One big emotional rollercoaster! – Tanya Figliozzi

Question: What is exactly the way you expected it?

I have trained non-service dog pups before, but the amount of awareness and connection we have with each other is deeper than I've had with any dog before. --Kaleb Kelly

Not much. I expected a perfect dog who never makes mistakes. Does all the tricks I want, and I barely have to have treats on me. I expected a dog who knows exactly when I'm going to have an anxiety attack any time of the day--even when she is away from me. That didn't happen. --River

The public. --Lauren Girsh

Really none of it. --Rose family

My service dogs have changed my life for the better and enabled me to do things I couldn't do before. I'm not sure it was an expectation so much as a hope. It definitely happened, but more so than I ever could have imagined. --Marleigh

I knew that everything was going to be brand-new for me, as I had never owned a dog before in my life, and I knew that I was going to have lots of moments of failure and frustration. Thankfully, I have tons of support whenever I have any training problems with Clover. --Sam

How close Valor and I are. I definitely expected a service dog to be by my side all the time, and he follows me around like a duckling. --Janet

How difficult it was. Training takes a great deal of time and commitment, and while I knew this upfront, it was another thing altogether to be thrown in the middle of it. (I started out owner-training and have moved to a started dog program as my disability worsened and made it harder to train). --Leonard Duncan

Nothing. --Kelsey

Question: If you could tell someone going into this anything about one of the biggest mistakes/missteps people make in how they approach getting a service dog, what would it be?

From FIGZ: *One of the biggest mistakes people make is not keeping the tasks that they need from the service dog as the driving factor in choosing a breed of dog. One must also look at their health restrictions before choosing a breed. Factors such* as sight, mobility, allergies, and any other limitations need to be included in the decision process. Not all breeds of dogs can perform all the tasks needed to do their service work. Getting a dog that isn't the right size or temperament or that sheds because one thinks they can work around those things almost always sets the team up for failure.

Once a breed has been chosen, each dog must be tested individually. Additionally, not all service dog candidates can perform all tasks needed to do their service work. For example, a diabetic alert dog needs to be a strong scenter, a PTSD support dog needs to be able to handle loud sounds and have a rock-solid temperament, and a mobility dog needs to be one-third to one-half of the size of their handler. Failing to pick the right dog within the right breed can also lead to the team not being successful.

The second biggest mistake is waiting too long to start training. Most programs want the dog to be at least 6 months old to start training. That's too late to start. We start working with our puppies as young as 3 days old. Once they go to their handler at 8-9 weeks of age, we expect training to continue from day one of being home. By waiting till 6 months of age, the handler loses the "sponge" phase where the dog can soak in so many life lessons quickly and easily. While dogs older than 6 months can successfully complete a service dog training program, it is much easier if started sooner.

Veterinarians will warn you, "Don't take your puppy anywhere until they have had all their shoots," due to the puppies' lack of immunity to diseases such as parvo, distemper, etc. Again, puppies will miss out on great learning opportunities and not get enough socialization if you wait. Just be safe about taking the puppy out. Stay out of dog parks or places where other dogs frequent. Keep puppies off the grass and dirt by carrying them in your arms, a basket, or a stroller. Limit other dog interactions to dogs that you know are safe (have had all their shots and do not go to parks with other dogs). Puppies need to meet all different *shapes, sizes, ages, and colors of people, some with facial hair, sunglasses, hats, piercings, and tattoos. The same goes for animals. Dogs should experience different breeds of dogs, cats, hamsters, rabbits, horses, goats, etc. Experience doesn't mean the dog needs to touch it or play with it. Simply seeing it can be enough.*

From Amanda: *The number one mistake is always the people who get a dog before they get a trainer because most dogs do not make it as service dogs. I get a lot of people who come and get temperament tests done, and I tell them right away, "This is not going to work out," and now they just have a dog that they don't need, and it's not ever going to be a service dog, but they want a service dog, and they need a service dog, but they don't want to get rid of the dog they have. So, do not get a dog before you get a trainer. Get a trainer, then get a dog. That is the best order you could ever go in; because your trainer needs to find your dog, temperament test it, and get you the right animal for your needs. And if you cannot find a trainer that has connections to breeders, or connections to rescues, then you're going to struggle a little bit more. So make sure your trainer has connections.*

Another thing that people don't do well when it comes to service dog training is life changes. If you have a big life change coming up, such as you're trying to have a baby, you're planning on moving, you have other things coming along that are going to take precedence over an animal, you should not be getting a service dog at this time. It is so easy to think that you can do it all; because, trust me, I wish I could do it all, and I want to do it all, but I know I can't. I know the feeling of thinking you can do it all. But, you can't; nobody can do it all, so you have to find those balances in your life; if you are not ready to take two years of your life, and dedicate it to something, then you're not ready for a service dog.

Question: If you could tell someone just starting on the service dog journey anything, what would it be?

It's HARD but worth it. Nothing happens overnight. But it will start to fall into place. --Rose family

Be patient; don't compare your journey to anyone else's. Each team is different and what's important is the health and happiness of you and your dog, not necessarily training. --Leonard Duncan

Be ready for the public; you can be rude! You will feel like a failure, but you aren't. Your dog will embarrass you A LOT. Have fun with training and just life in general with your dog. --Lauren Girsh

Always remember to take a breath, and remember, it's not going to be easy, but it's going to be worth it in the end. You're not gonna be at the pace that everyone else is. --Kelsey

Do. Your. Research. --Sam

Don't overwhelm yourself with too many goals at one time. It takes a long time, and honestly, they're always learning, so just enjoy the journey. --Anonymous

There is a saying in the service dog community that goes, "need Before breed," which essentially means thinking about what you will need from your service dog before just adopting or purchasing the first cute puppy you think would be a good prospective service dog. It may or may not work out for the specific needs that you have. --Janet

They will make mistakes. Take deep breaths and remember that. They aren't human; they are a dog. They don't understand why you are upset with them, so don't get angry when you find poop or something. The dog won't know what you are upset about unless you catch them in the act. --River

You can get better results with a treat than you can with a correction. --Kaleb Kelly

It's so, so hard, but, at least for me, it has been so worth it a thousand times over. --Marleigh

Question: If you could go back and redo anything on this journey, would you? If so, what would it be?

To work harder and try to attend more meetings. --Rose family

Wait until COVID is over to start training. I got JoJo right before it all hit, and it's made everything so much more difficult. --Leonard Duncan

Getting her sooner and having her as a puppy. --Lauren Girsh

Honestly, to do specific things that I didn't do at the beginning that I should have; it could've helped me where I'm at now--on our way to graduation. But, honestly, I would at least want my family to be more supportive and more involved instead of being judgmental. --Kelsey

Maybe I should have done a little more research about dealing with a pit bull, but besides that, absolutely not. --Sam

I would spend more time in the 8-16 week old range just bonding and training. --Anonymous

Nope, I love things the way they are. --Janet

I would go back and try to get my dog earlier. My dog's relationship with me--and a lot of her socializing--was not the best. As much as the company tried, a lot of puppy raisers were not the best for her. So, she is not the best at some things. I wish I could go back and form a better relationship with her and have her grow with me. --River

I would redo my concept of "accomplishment" with Roo. Accomplishment is not passing a lesson. It's progress; it's going backward to then move forward. It's the moment your dog GETS it. --Kaleb Kelly

All of my dogs have made me better; as a trainer, handler, and person, but a lot of things would've been easier if I'd been more educated about how to pick an appropriate prospect. My first dog was unnecessarily hard, and maybe if I'd been more educated on what to look for, he could've worked longer and without quite so much bedlam. --Marleigh

3. Service Dogs vs. Therapy Dogs vs. Emotional Support Dogs

Not everyone who thinks they need a service dog actually needs a service dog. Why is this? Because a lot of people misunderstand what the term "service dog" actually means. There are three types of working dogs that people tend to use interchangeably, which absolutely do not mean the same thing:

- Service dogs
- Emotional support dogs
- Therapy dogs

The term "service dog" has been expanded in the everyday vernacular to mean "a working dog," when that is attributing a wide array of dogs the title only a handful have earned. And, like using a term that two different parties define two different ways can hurt discussions and debates, using the term "service dogs" that loosely can hurt people in each of the above groups.

Service dogs are trained to perform specific jobs for one person to make the handler's life easier and take the difficulty level of their adventure down a step if you will. There is a unique partnership necessary to handle this type of dog.

Service dog training takes roughly two years and costs around $10,000.

Service dog handlers cannot be refused by landlords on the grounds of a "no pets" policy; in that way, they are medical equipment.

The only public places that can refuse service dogs entrance are places of worship and places that need to be completely immaculate--operating rooms and the kitchens of restaurants, for example.

Airlines cannot refuse service dogs from sitting with their people. This and restaurants are why "under" is a big skill to be practiced! The dog is trained to lie under the person's legs for extended periods of time. Airlines cannot charge extra for a service dog, and the traveler does not necessarily have to call ahead. If someone on the plane is allergic to dogs, the airline can only separate them as much as possible--neither can be kicked off for the sake of the other.

Service dogs have to be what my trainer calls bomb-proof. They cannot panic or spook in the heat of the moment. They cannot freak out because of another dog, a loud noise, or a lot of really good-smelling stuff when their human needs them to perform their service.

Service animals can only be a dog or, in special cases, miniature horses.

Service dogs do not require registration.

Therapy dogs are in the middle of the field of these working dogs. Therapy dogs have gone through basic obedience to serve large numbers of people--usually strangers. These are the ones you will see touring hospitals or nursing homes, the dogs children read to at libraries. Their main job is to be sweet and calm around those who are in stressful situations and give them that calm, peaceful feeling. You know the one, yes?

As I said, therapy dogs have gone through at least basic training and have a mellow, sociable personality.

Therapy dogs get no special allowances for housing. In the case of public buildings, they only get said special treatment if previously discussed with management in cases such as the above-mentioned.

Therapy dogs have to be well-behaved and calm around any of the kinds of people they will be working around--whether that's kids or elderly people; people who hide their turmoil well or wear it on their sleeve; people with hats or without; with backpacks and without; people of different races, different genders, all the things. Dogs don't generalize--to them, a person without a hat isn't necessarily the same thing as a person with a hat, and males smell different from females. Hispanic people look different from Native Americans, who look different from Albinos, so, to a dog, it's not an automatic given that these two people are in the same "group." Dogs are very breedist in their own groups, so why not with humans? This is why training around a wide variety of people is important for any dog in public--just because they're okay with everyone in your life doesn't mean they're okay with every person out there.

Any animal can be a therapy animal--I've seen pictures of therapy horses with cardboard horns; therapy unicorns! How cool is that?!

Emotional support animals (ESA) need no special training. They're like a therapy dog, for one--except they're not allowed in public.

Landlords and public travel cannot require you to pay more for an emotional support animal. However, as of December 2020, airlines are allowed to treat emotional support animals as pets--the only animals allowed to travel in the cabin fee-free are now service dogs. Non-pet-friendly housing will let emotional support animals slide--with a letter from your doctor saying you need one. Without a letter, they don't have to allow you to have an emotional support animal in a non-pet-friendly home.

Emotional support animals ARE NOT allowed anywhere normal pets aren't allowed. Period. (Breaking this rule is where you get the most 'fake service dogs'--something covered later.)

Emotional support animals can be any animal.

So, you see, when people refer to emotional support dogs as service dogs or service dogs as therapy dogs, it can actually hurt the handler, either by putting more expectations on the dog than they can live up to or discrediting how hard they are working and how well they are trained.

How do you know you need a service dog rather than an emotional support animal, time with a therapy dog, or just a pet?

Question: What made you consider a service dog?

Talking with someone who made me feel welcome and guided me to learn more about ways a service dog would help benefit my life. --Kaleb Kelly

It was recommended by my therapist after a while, realizing animals made me calmer and first getting an emotional support animal, but needing something more full-time to help me not have so many anxiety attacks. --River

Being in the hospital and having a life threat of disease that has no cure. --Lauren Girsh *Our son Abel is a full-time wheelchair user.* --Rose family

I had been thinking about having a service dog for about a year and a half before getting Clover through Scout's Legacy Service Dogs. I knew that medication and therapy alone weren't going to help me completely mitigate my disabilities enough to the point where I could function normally in a public environment. So, I explored other options, which led me to consider getting a service dog heavily. --Sam

I wasn't able to leave the house without someone else coming with me. --Janet

My disabilities started to become more severe, and as a young adult without a family to help me, I worried about my quality of life as an independent student. --Leonard Duncan

It was my last option; medications haven't helped, and it's made a lot of things hard in my life. --Kelsey

Seemingly uncontrollable OCD and anxiety. --Anonymous

What do you need a service dog to be trained for? Seizure response? Diabetes alert? PTSD response? Counterweight?

If you need a service dog, I'm guessing you already know--it's not like it's that hard to figure out where your life isn't "normal," right? Where could you use a consistent helping hand?

If you're not sure, ask yourself why you're looking for a service dog; if you are looking for a service dog.

Question: As someone very deep in the dog world on the whole, can you share your thoughts on service dogs v therapy dogs v emotional support dogs?

From Amanda: *Legal definition of a service dog is an animal that is task-trained to help--not just an animal, but it's a dog or miniature horse--who is task trained to help someone with a disability. They work for one person, and they help that one person--they're just with their person.*

A therapy dog is an animal that is basic obedience trained and has a quality temperament to be able to go into places such as hospitals, nursing homes, and schools to provide comfort to other people. They are owned by someone, but that owner does not use them for themselves as a therapy dog. They take them places to provide therapy to other people.

And, then, lastly, emotional support dogs. An ESA can actually be any animal. ESAs are not restricted to just dogs. You can have an emotional support (ES) guinea pig, or you can have an ES fish. But it's just any animal that provides comfort. That way, those with psychiatric disabilities who can handle it in public can find a zen or channel their psychiatric disability into their animal in their own private home. With a letter from your psychiatrist, ESAs are required to be allowed to live in non-pet-friendly housing. So it's not a certification thing. Again, it is your letter from your doctor saying you need an emotional support animal.

ESAs are also not required to be trained, which is why they do not get public access rights. They are just a pet. And, to the entire world, they're just another pet. But, to that one person, they are their livelihood and their life. An ESA needs to be out there in the world, but, it is also important for people to understand that if you need more than just a pet, then you should look into a service dog--not an ESA, because ESAs are just, go to pet-friendly places, you just do your own thing, you cuddle at home, and all that jazz; but, they don't go into public places with you.

From Tanya of FIGZ: *It is important to understand that there are 3 sets of rules when it comes to the differences between service dogs, therapy dogs, and emotional support dogs.*

1. *Americans with Disabilities Act (ADA), along with federal, state, and local governments, that deal with discrimination*
2. *Fair Housing which deals with these animals in housing situations*
3. *The U.S. Department of Transportation (Department of DOT) issued a final rule to amend the Department's Air Carrier Access Act (ACAA). ACAA deals with these animals on an airline.*

ADA: As of March 15, 2011, titles II and III of the Americans with Disabilities Act (ADA) under The U.S. Department of Justice Civil Rights Division, along with federal, state, and local governments which will deal with discrimination, define a service animal as any breed and any size of dog trained to perform a task directly related to a person's disability. They allow the service dog to accompany people with disabilities in all areas where members of the public are allowed to go. Service animals are not something other than a dog. They are not emotional support or comfort dogs because providing emotional support or comfort is not a task related to a person's disability. Nor are they required to be certified or go through a professional training program or required to wear a vest or other ID that indicates they're a service dog.

When it is not obvious what service an animal provides, staff may ask two questions: (1) is the dog a service animal required because of a disability, and (2) what work or task has the dog been trained to perform? Staff cannot ask about the person's disability, require medical documentation, require a special identification card or training documentation for the dog, or ask that the dog demonstrate its ability to perform the work or task.

A person with a disability cannot be asked to remove his service animal from the premises unless: (1) the dog is out of control and the handler does not take effective action to control it or (2) the dog is not housebroken.

HUD: According to The U.S. Department of Housing and Urban Development, an assistance animal is an animal that works, provides assistance, or performs tasks for the benefit of a person with a disability or that provides emotional support that alleviates one or more identified effects of a person's disability. An assistance animal is not a pet but DOES NOT need to be a service animal. HUD is the only department that offers protection to emotional support or comfort animals.

ACAA: On December 20, 2020, The U.S. Department of Transportation (Department or DOT) issued a final rule to amend the Department's Air Carrier Access Act (ACAA) regulation on the transport of service animals by air, which became effective as of January 11, 2021. This final rule defines a service animal as a dog, regardless of breed or type, that is individually trained to do work or perform tasks for the benefit of a qualified individual with a disability, including a physical, sensory, psychiatric, intellectual, or other mental disability. It allows airlines to recognize emotional support animals as pets rather than service animals and permits airlines to limit the number of service animals that one passenger can bring onboard an aircraft to two service animals.

The final rule also allows airlines to require passengers with a disability traveling with a service animal to complete and submit to the airline a form developed by DOT up to 48 hours in advance of the date of travel. It better ensures the safety of passengers and crew members by allowing airlines to require that service animals are harnessed, leashed, or otherwise tethered onboard an aircraft. Further, it specifies the circumstances under which the user of a service animal may be charged for damage caused by the service animal on the aircraft.

However, the final rule prohibits airlines from requiring passengers to physically check in at the airport solely on the basis that the individual is traveling with a service animal, thus ensuring that service animal users are not prevented from enjoying the same convenience-related benefits provided to other passengers.

Foot Two:

Training

1. Systems

There are several different ways to get a trained service dog. Not all of them require an organization to learn through.

There's the best-known way of just buying a fully trained dog--something for which the price can be somewhere between a decent, used car and a new, shiny one. With this solution, you pay a butt-load of cash, join a waiting list, and hope the dog is trained for your specific needs and that you bond well.

With this, you will have a few things on the back end to work with the dog on, just to connect all the wires, communication, and all. The large bulk of training, however, happens in those two years you're on the waiting list, and you largely end up with completed training.

You're part of the just-in-time posse that shows up to aid the group of heroes at the very end of the story and save the day.

You could also do what I did and owner-train. This is a training solution that falls squarely on the handler's shoulders. The group we are a part of--Scout's Legacy--takes place largely through Facebook and did even before the COVID-19 pandemic shutdowns. Training takes place at home, in public, and in a handful of group training each month, with the handler taking charge of the speed and intensity each day, with the supervision and advice of a trainer. The trainer will sometimes step in to work with a dog to see where they are and/or show the handler how to do a specific task, but their job is largely to train the handler on how to train the dog.

In the allegory of an adventure, you start from the very beginning and see it all the way through. You are the one who starts the adventure and--often miraculously, in the world of stories--are also able to see it completed. Owner training with the mentorship of a trainer is a fairly new system.

There is also a solution that falls in between these two: puppy raising. This is a solution, mainly to puppyhood. A volunteer (that has to be either inhuman or surely doing penance for something) brings home the puppy and trains through housebreaking, teething fear, and adolescent stages. When the dog is more mature, they are passed on to its handlers, who take over training from there.

This is kind of like a "cheat code" in the world of service dog training, starting the adventure at some point halfway through the thirteen-year walk. You're not getting off easy, but you only have aching feet for the second half.

There are several other systems of training, as well. I'm not going to go into them here, however. These are the three systems I know the most about, and I don't want to steer any of you wrong, trying to explain what I don't know. :) The point is, this isn't a one-size-fits-all system, just like most of the other stuff in the service dog world.

I just want to take a moment here to give a shout-out to any and all puppy raisers and non-owner-trainers because their jobs are *hard*. Personally, if I weren't getting a fully trained dog at the end, I couldn't go through the puppy phases. It's not easy when I *get* the dog at the end. So, to all of you who do that out of the goodness of your heart... *THANK YOU!!*

Question: What advice do you have on deciding on a method of training (owner, puppy raiser, fully trained, etc.)?

From FIGZ: *How the dog is trained is 100% reliant on the ability of the handler and the accessibility of a training program. This is where you, the handler, have to be completely honest with yourself.*

For a train-your-own service dog, do you have the time needed to train the dog multiple times a day, every day of every week, every week of every month, and every month for the next 2 years? It takes hundreds, if not thousands, of training hours to fully train a service dog. The length of training will depend on the tasks needed. For example, a mobility assistance dog should not start any weight-bearing training until the dog is approximately 18-24 months of age after the dog's growth plates have closed and the dog has matured in size. For scent-working dogs, such as seizure alert, training time could depend on the number of seizures the handler has. The service dog not only needs to be trained on how to respond to a seizure, but the scent also needs to be paired with the handler. If the handler is experiencing less than normal amounts of seizures, it could take longer to train the dog.

For a partially- or fully-trained service dog, do you have the money needed? Some disabilities may not allow the handler the ability to train their own dog. In such cases, a person may need a partially- or fully-trained service dog. In these situations, someone other than the handler will be doing countless hours of training. This comes at a price. I have found that Board and Train organizations charge anywhere from $2,800 - $5,000 per month. Just like different boarding facilities, these training facilities will have different levels of comfort and interaction for the dogs. For the most part, the dog will live in a kennel, only being let out to train, play, and potty. After the basic training has been completed, there will still be a period of time when the dog now has to be paired with the handler, and the handler and dog need to learn to work together. If the dog needs 18 months of training, the dog will cost over $43,000.

We have found that our highest success rate is with the Train-Your-Own program. With the Train-Your-Own program, a trainer is paid to provide lessons, evaluate homework, be available to answer training questions and help handle any issues. Train-Your-Own programs will generally cost about $10,000 over a 2-year period.

From Amanda: *Owner training is a thing that a lot of people like because they get to have the dog in their home right away, and they get to be part of the process. It is a great thing for a lot of people who want to save money. You spend the same amount of money; you're just not dropping all of it at one time; it is over a longer time frame. So, for a lot of people, it's just, financially, an easier outlet.*

Owner training is also beneficial because of that bond with a dog. Later on, when you're working as a fully trained team, it's great because you knew exactly what this dog did as a puppy and how you got through it, and sometimes they refer back to that stage, so you're like, "hey, this worked then, we're going to do it again," and you're able to work through it quicker.

A fully trained dog is something that many people need that think they want to do owner training, unfortunately. If you are not prepared to take the time to work these young dogs the way they need to, then you don't need to owner-train. And I say that with all the love in my heart. I really do. With owner training, I get a lot of people who are gung-ho; but they don't get their homework in, they don't get to outings, and they don't get to the group training. If you're not doing that--and you're not prepared to do that--you're not going to succeed as a team. Meanwhile, I do have clients who do great at it; those owner-training teams are fabulous, and I have no problems with them. But, if you're not prepared to put the work in and maybe take out something in your life to focus on this for a couple of years, then owner training may not be for you.

Now, with a fully trained dog, you have a little bit of the advantage of knowing that you don't have to take on a dog that's going to wash, and that's the biggest pro when it comes to fully trained; you have a dog who you know is good to go as a service dog. While your owner is training teams, they may run into a washed dog because, again, not every dog is meant for this job. With your fully trained team, your dog already has a lot of the understanding, but the problem with fully trained is the fact that these dogs know more than you, so you have a lot of catching up to do. You have to work twice as hard to get to the same level that your dog is at, and if your dog figures out that you don't know as much as them, they are going to walk all over you. When you do run into trouble, you're going to run into not knowing how to get through it unless you have the trainer's help. Not a problem with our company. I'm here to help, but some companies are not as helpful as others, so you do have to realize that you're going to need help; you need that full-time support, you need that backup from your trainer, so be sure you have a company that is there for you after graduation.

2. Trainers

This is one of, if not the most important thing in your service dog journey. If your dog is perfect--which it won't be, but say that it is--but you don't have a good trainer, the dog won't mean much. If your dog is a hot mess--which they all are now and again, but you have a good trainer, you will pull through it in one way or another. Even if that means the answer you get is that the way you pull through this is by acknowledging this isn't the path for your dog.

There will be several things to look out for in a trainer and a training program cropping up naturally in the following pages, but there are some I want to start you off with, going from my personal experience.

--Prompt responses

The organization I am working with right now was not the first one we reached out to. That one, however, didn't respond to my reaching out or questions for months. This is not good. When you're in the program, if you have an urgent question, you want to be able to know they will respond quickly. Your dog's health could very well depend on the answers they give you. This also applies to breeders.

This happened to us recently. Cor was acting strange-- unable to lie down and rest, sniffing the edges of the room, and walking all hunched up. When we let him out to go potty, he'd trot around looking for a spot, but then he wouldn't try to go. He'd just lie down and stare at us.

Looking back on it, we should've known something was off. Unfortunately, it took us a while to realize it. We reached out to our breeders and asked if they had thoughts as to what was going on.

They brought up two options: bloat or a blockage. Each of these would be enough to send us on an emergency vet run at ten on a Saturday night.

Was there anything we could do?

If we acted quickly, maybe. Run to the nearest drugstore and pick up a Gas-X and a Pepcid. Take six of those tablets and shove them down his throat for the bloat. In case it is a blockage, pick up some Karo syrup or honey, and get him to take a tablespoon of that. Get a good amount on your finger and smear it on the roof of his mouth. He won't like any of this, but if we're early enough, it may work. At that point, rub his belly like so.

We wanted to look for any gas release, belly gurgles, or softening of his distended abdomen. Also, if he looked easier and more comfortable, that was good. If there were no changes in ten minutes, take him to the animal hospital immediately.

The changes came. They started a handful of seconds after we gave him the Gas-X and Pepcid and just kept coming.

We still slept lightly that night, and I mean that in two senses of the word--I was instantly alert if he moved, and we slept with the light on so I could easily check on him.

This is why quick responses from a breeder and trainer are important. If we hadn't gotten them from our breeders, we likely would've ended up with a $2500 emergency vet bill... or worse.

This is also why you want to be in close contact with them. We're new at this; we don't know what we don't know, and no book is going to be able to prepare you for everything you'll encounter.

Note: breeders and trainers are humans, too. They get busy. By "prompt response," I don't mean that they're sitting on the phone, ready to answer the second a text comes through, but you shouldn't have to wait a week between texts.

--Willing to work with you beyond graduation

Training is a life-long adventure. You can't rest on your laurels after graduation. You will have more questions, and you will need more answers. You will need to continue challenging your dog and reviewing the basics. If they throw a fit, you need to be able to get feedback on how to handle it. Your work doesn't stop after graduation, so your partnership with your trainer can't stop after graduation.

--Positive reviews from people who have fully trained dogs through this trainer--these don't have to be official reviews, but you want to find people who have been through the training program and speak well of the graduated dogs.

Puppyhood is not nearly as cute as those going through it, and the majority of training takes place during this difficult time. There are some handlers that don't obey as well as even the most hard-headed dogs. Because of this, there are some handlers that are told they have to either shape up or leave the program they're in. There are other programs that won't take certain handlers or dogs or that don't train specific types of service dogs.

You can find negative reviews on anything, from whatever president or monarch is in power to Mother Theresa. Negative sells and it's very easy for people to be negative when they don't have a firm understanding of the situation at hand. You don't want to take advice on something like this from just any old Joe. Some people may be predisposed to hate just to cause conflict, or others may have had a negative experience because of something they did but spit vitriol at the trainer because they don't want to admit they did something wrong.

If you're going to listen to advice on which organization to go with--and I highly suggest you do--make sure that those you're taking advice from know what they're talking about. The best people to take advice from, in this case, are people who are deep in the world. The best way to do this is to talk to those who know what the completely trained dogs from an organization are like because they deal with them every day--are they easily spooked? How extensive was their training? What problems have they run into? Do you know how long they are able to work before retirement, on average?

--Connections in the dog world

This is very much like finding a breeder. You want them to know the dog world, to have worked within it a lot so that they know how to coach you through the ups and downs. You want to be able to go to them for answers. You also want a trainer that has connections to breeders and rescues, who can give advice on how to get a good puppy, and who will admit the less lovely aspects of the dog world.

Question: As someone very deep in the dog world on the whole, can you share your thoughts on what to look for in a service dog trainer?

From Amanda: *This one is my biggest pet peeve because there are just so many trainers out there, and, honestly, it's not a one-trainer-fits-all type of deal. There are some great ones out there that I don't like, and there are some bad ones out there that I don't like. I mean, it's just... it is what it is. The industry is not controlled. And so, because it's not controlled, you have a whole bunch of people who think they're doing good but aren't, or who just like to bad mouth other people but don't like to work their animals. So, when you're looking for a service dog trainer, I always tell people to first look at timelines. If someone tells you that they can get your dog trained in six months or less, run away. That is someone who is either not fully training your animal or is training it to an extent where it's not going to be able to work for a long period of time, and it's gonna shut down on you.*

The second thing about service dog trainers, you want to look for someone who you can fully trust. Because if you are talking to someone and you don't have trust in that person, you are never going to be able to train your dog with them. You have to be able to understand when you're being told you're doing right and when you're being told you're doing wrong. And then you have to be able to take those words and trust your trainer and follow through with what they're asking of you. If you don't trust them, or you don't feel like they're the right fit for you, that is fine. Not every trainer is meant for everyone, so find the person that does work for you.

Any place that will give you a certification for your service dog is usually a scam site. There are plenty of organizations out there that'll train your dog in a very short time frame and then certify it, give you all the certificates, and say, "You're a service dog now, congrats. Go off and be merry." Those usually aren't going to be quality service dog programs. The other thing is you always want a program that's willing to back up your dog after graduation. Unfortunately, our dogs are not robots; they're going to have problems when they're fully trained service dogs because, again, they're not robots. You have to be able to have the support system after your dog is fully graduated, or else you're never going to make it as a team for the rest of its career.

Lastly, look into people who have dogs that have graduated or have been with the program for a long period of time, and talk with them about the ups and downs of the program. No program is perfect--every trainer has grown and has strengths and weaknesses, and every trainer has made mistakes. There will be times when you're going to hear stories or trainers are just the worst in some people's minds. Everyone has enemies in the training world. The dog world is not always the nicest, so it's one of those find the stories you need to find to make yourself feel comfortable with moving forward or find the stories you need to find to say no; but just remember, each person has their own choices, so you have to figure out what works best for you at the end of the day.

Foot Three:

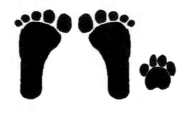

Mindset

1. The Public

"Do not pet."
"Working--please leave us alone."
"No touch, no talk, no eye contact."
I have seen all of these patches on service dog vests. Because people need to be reminded that being distracted can be a matter of life and death. Is it, most of the time? No, but all it takes is one time. And, to be honest, it's not just for our safety, either. You don't know my dog; we may be working on him not viciously attacking strangers. Granted, if we were, we likely wouldn't be in public, but you don't know where his line is. Politeness doesn't mean we mean it any less than some patches I've seen that tell you to do so in much firmer words--a couple even using some more colorful language when telling you to step off. Kindness doesn't mean pliable boundaries; curse words may not just be a facade or for shock value.

He is my dog. He is my best friend. I trust him more than anyone else in my life simply because I have to. When he has the vest on, we have to be one creature with six legs, not a girl and her dog. We have to be able to unwaveringly place our life in the other's control at any given moment because that's why I have a service dog.

I cannot simply see him as medical equipment to be used when I need him and then stored away for later. He is a live, flesh-and-blood creature. When the vest is off, he has to be able to be a puppy. To make mistakes, play, and be imperfect. He may be medical equipment, but he isn't like an oxygen tank or a walker in that you can store them away.

At the same time, he may be a flesh-and-blood creature, but he is like an oxygen tank or a walker in that you wouldn't walk up to someone and shut the valve of their oxygen tank off or take their walker for a spin, would you?

And yet... people will walk up to Cor and start petting him without asking. (I wish I was joking--I have had strangers tell others they can pet him when they didn't even ask to. If nothing else, having a service dog has done wonders for my ability to talk to strangers.)

This is why service dogs need to be bomb-proof. If you walk up to a dog on a walk and just start petting them, what do they do? Get all happy and waggy and nearly fall over themselves, showing you their belly, right? ...Unless they attack you because you're a stranger that walked up and randomly started messing with their hair. In the human world, we call that sexual harassment.

Anyway... have you ever seen a service dog--an actual service dog--get all waggy and happy? Heck no. Why? Because they can't. A random passerby may walk up and start petting and cooing over how well-behaved he is, how fluffy he is, and asking if he is a labradoodle. What does Cor do? He has to focus on me as I smile and answer that yes, he is well-behaved because we've worked on that, and yes, he is fluffy because he's a standard poodle, but he's working right now (hence the vest), so he can't be petted at the moment. But, even if I tell them they can't pet him, they already have petted him; the damage is already done.

I have petite mal seizures. Therefore, I cannot drive and will likely have someone with me when we're out while he's still in training so that even if Cor did get distracted, several things align that make it so it wouldn't be a life and death situation. But they don't know that.

What if I had grand mal seizures or diabetes that needed split-second attention? PTSD? Anxiety? What if my dysautonomia was worse than it is, and while they were petting him, and he was falling all over himself to show his belly, my monster decided to rear its head? If Cor was distracted by people petting and cooing over him and missed a cue that I need him--now, and I ended up hurt or worse... that's why people shouldn't pet service dogs.

I've been on both sides of it--I know how hard it is to ignore that doggy face. I know how your human nature goes, "Cute!!! MUST PET!" and yet... if the dog knows what "leave it" means, why don't humans? But, for some reason, they don't. And that has driven people who need service dogs to choose not to get them because the attention they get in public--the inability to ever be invisible again--is so nerve-wracking and life-altering that they'd rather deal with the certainty of not having the help.

The importance of not petting or distracting a service dog is one of the large and many misconceptions the general public has about service dogs. These are things you will undoubtedly run into on your adventure of training, raising, or getting a service dog. Everyone runs into this challenge, as well as a handful of others. For this reason, I have opened this question to people I know in this world and decided to just share the answers here:

Question: What, in your mind, is the biggest misconception the general public has about service dog life in general?

I think a lot of people don't understand how hard it is, not just training but how inconvenient it can be to have to take a dog everywhere with you. They also don't seem to be aware of invisible disabilities or the fact that stopping someone to ask them questions isn't appropriate. A lot of people also don't know that owner training exists, the price tag of a fully trained service dog, or how long it takes them to get there. --Marleigh

The biggest misconception about living with a service dog is that it makes your life so much easier and that it's the "cure-all." And, for some reason, people see these animals out in public, and they see these people living a much more normal life, and they think, "Oh, I want that; I want a normal life," so they get into it--thinking it's going to be easy, and it's not. This is one of the hardest things that people can do for their disability, and it's

nonstop. After your dog graduates, you're still working. You're still training, and you're still doing things to make sure that the dog and you are a perfect team. This is a lifetime training; this is not a two-year training, and then you're done, and you have a dog. It is a lifetime of work, so, in that sense, this is something that makes people go, "Oh, this is a lot more work than it should've been."
--Amanda

Most service dogs are not working 24/7; when their vest is off, they are free to play and enjoy life. Service dogs are not robots. They have good and bad days. Some will even have temper tantrums like toddlers. It is important for a handler to know it is OKAY to excuse oneself and the service dog and take a "time out". If you are having a bad day, sometimes it is best to stop and just try again tomorrow. –FIGZ

The misconception is:

Service dogs are perfect dogs that never make mistakes.
--Leonard Duncan

That you have to have a visible disability to have a service dog. --Lauren Girsh

Just because you see a dog, you can touch it without the owner's approval or consequences. That we have our dogs because they're pets--yes, but only to a point. Reality is, yes, a dog is a pet, but that doesn't mean that we have our pet out in public just for the heck of it--we have our service dogs with us because they are our lifeline; we have something wrong with us that makes us disabled and makes us need a little extra assistance that humans or meds sometimes can't provide. --Kelsey

Dogs that help people with invisible disabilities are not valid. And that psychiatric service dogs and ESAs are the same things. --Sam

That you need to make a comment about my dog. Just ignore him. We're fine. --Anonymous

That there is a service dog registry/registration. That is one of the biggest scams I hear about and is always one of the best ways to know if a service dog is fake or not. --Janet

That the dogs are perfect dogs who never make a mistake when they are fully trained. Dogs who are fully trained still make mistakes. --River

We are all broken or have visible disabilities. --Kaleb Kelly

People don't know: That they can just be regular dogs. --Rose family

That they do not have rights to your dog--they need to leave you alone. --Lauren Girsh

2. Guilt

As I'm sure you were able to find in previous sections, there is a large problem that I easily fall into with beating myself up over things that either aren't within my control or that simply won't be fixed by relying on that specific tactic. This is something that, as I said, is very easy to fall into--too easy, really--and it trips a lot of people up in normal day-by-day stuff, and even more so when you're raising a dependent or trying to bring out the best in someone via training.

Have you heard of mama guilt? Well, dog handler guilt (I am stubbornly avoiding being called a dog mom) is a very real thing.

Why? Because bullying yourself never gets anyone anywhere, and that's very much what this is--you are bullying yourself over something you either have no control over or something that would benefit from the energy you are devoting to bullying yourself being put toward fixing it. Also, your dog can tell how you're feeling, so if you get frustrated, it's very easy for them to get frustrated and nervous, which very quickly sends training into a downward spiral.

I am saying this as someone who is still learning and working through it. I am saying this as someone sitting in Wisconsin with my puppy twelve hundred miles away, wondering if I had let other people work with him before and if he'd be with me right now. If I wouldn't depend on him not wearing out his welcome with my family. Wondering how soon they'll start to feel like I'm shirking my responsibility of caring for my dog. I wonder this even as I know that I'm not throwing responsibility to the wind. Yet, it's still so easy for that little lying voice of guilt to whisper to me and get me to beat myself up for it. I already have enough work on my plate to stay fiscally responsible for Cor. I don't need to take on somebody else's work, and yet, it's something that comes so easily to me, and I give in far too often.

I am saying this as someone who has lived a little over eighteen years without a dog helping me and twenty-one years without a fully trained service dog. Do you know why? Because I had a family that was, effectively, my service humans. I had belt loops to slide my finger through in lieu of holding on to a guide handle. I had a family that when I suddenly woke up in the middle of a store with no idea where I was and no sign of the people I was there with, would recognize what had happened fairly quickly and retrace their steps. I knew all I had to do was stay where I woke up, and they'd find me.

I had classmates who, on our way down to lunch, would put a hand on my arm or shoulder and keep me moving if I had a seizure. I had classmates who would keep me from walking into walls and knew to just wait a few seconds if I trailed off in the middle of an answer. And when there was a bit of bullying behind my back that I wasn't aware of until years afterward, I had friends who would stand up for me, even though I wasn't aware of it. I had teachers who, regardless of how I felt, did know that this wasn't me not paying attention and would've repeated what they were teaching if I had ever summoned enough courage to ask.

As I said, I had service humans. I had learned how to live in pseudo-harmony with my seizures. As I became an adult, though, that wasn't going to be able to stay the same. I wasn't going to be able to depend so heavily on friends and family anymore, as I was going to be bouncing around, moving out, and doing who-knows-what-else. Transferring responsibility to a dog, then, made sense. But I hadn't needed one up until that point, so I also dealt quite a bit with the guilt of, "But do I really need it, though?" and the guilt of, "Maybe I'm lying to myself--maybe I'm unconsciously looking for attention and don't need the help and support."

If any of this sounds familiar, listen to me, friend--we're all living a different adventure than those who don't need service dogs--we're different, and there's no escaping it. But hear me, friend, that doesn't mean that what makes us different is inherently bad or wrong. It is what it is, and it is your special obstacle in this adventure.

I have never read an adventure where the hero didn't have some obstacle they needed to overcome, some villain they needed to fight. Do you know why? Because those stories are boring. Your story isn't boring, friend. People love to hear stories about overcoming obstacles and challenges. Your story is up there with the greats. Just because this adventure is different, leading to you needing different sidekicks and mentors and allies than many you know, doesn't mean it is any less valid.

3. Washing

In any adventure, there is the danger of ambushes or traps that you won't make it out of. Service dog training is no exception. In this case, though, it's no monster that you can fight off with a magic sword or whatever is your weapon of preference. Rather, it's the chance your dog will wash--something that you simply get to avoid, and the only way to do so is by listening to the wisdom of those you asked to teach you--your trainers.

It's like being in a giant corn maze and having someone on the lookout tower who can tell you how to get to where you're aiming for. You ignore their advice and instructions at your own peril.

Question: If you could tell someone going into this anything about washing, what would it be?

From FIGZ: *Washing can happen at any time during or after training and for a multitude of reasons. Some teams may never learn "The Dance," working together as one to flow through life as if dancing. Some handlers need a different dog. Some dogs succeed when paired with a different handler. It's kind of like a marriage. Two individually great people may be horrible together. It is important to always be your dog's advocate. If the dog is overwhelmed in a situation or if a person or another dog is acting inappropriately towards the handler or dog, it is the handler's responsibility to remove the dog from the situation so the dog doesn't have a lasting negative association with those things bothering it. The handler needs to understand there is no guarantee a dog will graduate from a service dog program. The handler must also understand there will come a time when a service dog will need to retire due to age, injury, health, or behavioral issues. A service dog who bites another dog or human should be immediately deemed washed and should stop working since it has been determined to be unfit for public access. Be honest with yourself and your dog. If things are not working out with continued training or the dog doesn't enjoy working, it is time to consider washing. You may need to find another dance partner.* [This is why Yaha washed if you remember.]

From Amanda: *Washing a service dog happens to more people than not. When you wash a service dog, you are saying that this dog is not able to fully make it as a service dog during their training process. That means that they never actually became a full-service dog; instead, they were either placed into a pet home or remained as a pet in their owner's home. When you wash a service dog, it just means that they don't have the temperament, the trainability, or the style to make it as a service dog.*

Washing is going to happen to more people than anyone wishes it would. Dogs are animals; they are not robots. They're going to go through all the stages that they're supposed to--the fear stages, the adolescent stages, and everything like that. When we discuss washing service dogs, we always want to make sure that people understand it is a possibility, and it is a high probability when you're owner training; because when you're working with a dog, and you don't know what you're doing, sometimes we make mistakes as humans, other times it is the dog itself.

Temperament testing is a great indicator to help, but there are a lot of things that pop up later in the dog's life for their instincts and genetic predispositions that don't show up in a temperament test, so we always tell people, really look at the history of a dog, their background, and everything like that to try and get a better idea of not washing a dog. But it will probably happen the first time.

When I started this adventure, I didn't realize this was even a real, concerning option. I knew in the back of my mind that it happened sometimes, but I had no idea how often it happened until I saw it happening in my rearview mirror, as it were. I would vaguely notice that I hadn't seen a particular dog at group outings in a while, and wasn't that person their handler? Maybe that person was a puppy raiser, and the dog had been passed on to its handler. That was all the thought I gave it until Amanda brought the possibility up with Yaha.

Slowly, the absence of those dogs came into stark relief, and the other option for what had happened loomed as large as a tsunami. Maybe they hadn't moved on... maybe the monster along the path had had its way.

Clearly, this doesn't happen with every dog. But it is a very real possibility, and the chance of this happening is something that needs to be seen because there is a chance of it happening. A very real chance. That said, when it happens, it doesn't inherently mean that the handler or the dog did anything wrong.

I refer back to Yaha. Yes, part of the problem was that he was being overprotective while we were in public, but that's only a problem because of the service dog he was training to be. As a psychiatric service dog, maybe that wouldn't have been as much of a deal breaker.

His fear stage and hormones were also more than he could handle--he didn't know what to do with himself, and being in public was stressing him out. That was by no means something he was doing wrong. That wasn't his fault, and it wasn't mine. We were trying to make it work--both of us.

To be a service dog is a big job. The simple fact is that not all dogs can do it. The temperament test when they're younger tells you whether it's worth trying to train them, but there's nothing that can guarantee who will make it through.

So if your dog washes and doesn't make it through the training program, listen to me.

It is not your fault.
It is not the dog's fault.
It happens.

Family who may be reading this?

Don't be jerks--if the handler was listening to the trainer, and--trust me--there is no motivation to not do so, it is not their fault.

I feel like I shouldn't have to say that, but apparently, there are some people who don't get this, so I guess I do.

The goal of everyone involved is to match the right dog to the handler that needs them. No one has been working against this goal at any point. Sometimes things like this just don't work out, as much as it hurts--because you have been working with this dog for as long as you have. Teams like this, by nature, are very intimate. You depend on each other and become one creature rather than two. To tear that apart isn't supposed to feel good.

If you are pulled into this pit, hear me, friend. You are justified in your pain. It is understandable, and you are not the first to have been here. Let yourself mourn for the partner you have lost, but--I beg you--don't shut yourself off from the next puppy. Don't sabotage yourself by shutting down or trying to shut your feelings off.

Your dog will come.

Your pain is justified.

4. Surprises

In spite of the danger and gloom you often run into on adventures, there are many times easier stretches in the journey. Bits of normalcy and space to breathe for the heroes so that it doesn't get so overbearingly dark no one can stomach to read or watch further. These often come as pleasant surprises, and--you know where I'm going with this by now--the service dog journey is no different.

One of these bits of space to breathe, which was a big surprise for me, and, I imagine, several others, is the service dog community.

Bit of a disclaimer here: I haven't gone deeper into the community than our training organization's little family. This is because it is very easy for it to get negative--for the love of chocolate, we all qualify as "disabled" for one or more reasons.

How many people keep a good perspective in spite of that, though, and the camaraderie and support of those who get what you're going through... that surprised me.

Again, it is easy to get negative. And, on behalf of everyone else, please *resist. The. Temptation.* It's alright to get down, but I and everyone else in the community *beg* you--don't give in to the toxic side because it's very real. As was brought up before, the dog world as a whole isn't always the most loving community.

Question: How important is the service dog community to your training experience?

Points scored

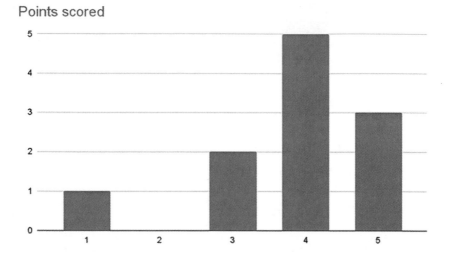

Question: Care to expound?

I think Scout's community has become extremely important to me, but outside Scout's community, I could mostly do without it. --Kaleb Kelly (4)

I have gotten help through the service dog community, but, at other turns, the service dog community has shot me down or yelled at me for something stupid because they didn't understand why we were doing it that way. --River (3)

I trained two other service dogs before Juno. One passed away from a heart defect, and the other retired. Juno is my first to have through an organization, and I have a better understanding of her training and know I'm not alone. I have people outside of my family who understand and want to see us succeed. --Lauren Girsh (5)

I want to make a distinction here - the community within Scout's Legacy specifically is amazing and really helps everyone with their journey, even those who've been through it before. When I was training my first dog, the service dog community as a whole was invaluable, and I don't think I could've made it without it; however, it has changed a lot since then and has become a very judgmental and negative place overall. --Marleigh (4)

I am very new to this community, and support for me is a very important factor in any relationship. Without this community of handlers, I don't know how I would be able to make it through owner training by myself. --Sam (4)

Despite how much I may have learned regarding reputable sources for my gear, the service dog community has a lot of toxic drama that I simply don't involve myself in for the sake of my own mind. --Janet (1)

If I were doing this alone, I would've given up a long time ago. --Leonard Duncan (5)

The friends I have made that understand me, my dog, and our training gives me relief knowing I'm not alone and others understand. --Kelsey (5)

Of course, there are other surprises. As with anything, you come into this with certain expectations, and you quickly realize things aren't always (or even most of the time), what you expect.

Question: What did you expect from a service dog that didn't happen?

How fast it would happen. --Rose family

Being able to have a dog come with me anywhere from minute one. --Leonard Duncan

The respect and knowledge from other people that they are a required medical "device." --Anonymous

That I would be able to train Valor quickly and smoothly without any bumps in the road, but the truth is, I have multiple disabilities that hinder me along the way, and my journey is different from everyone else's. It may take a little longer, but that doesn't mean I am worse. --Janet

Freedom. I expected that my life would open up with so many possibilities, and all I have met with are ableism and issues.

You get more freedom than you had with your illness, but not with the world. --River

I (foolishly) expected her to just KNOW what I needed. --Kaleb Kelly

A lot of people expect or assume that, especially with psych dogs, the dog takes the place of medication or people don't need their meds anymore once they have the dog--like they're mutually exclusive--which isn't necessarily true. Yes, some people are able to come off of some or all of their meds when they get a service dog, and others aren't. I needed both. My dog is part of my treatment plan that involves him, therapy, and medication; because that's what works for me. I did expect people to be more educated about how to act around a service dog or at least be able to read "do not pet" on the vest and know what that means, but apparently, that was wrong. --Marleigh

Foot Four:

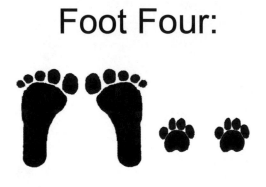

The Dog Itself

1. Preparing for Puppy

At this point, you're starting to get the idea of how big of a commitment this is, yes? I had done research into the requirements my trainer and breeder were going to expect from me--the things I was going to have to do, to sign, send in, promise, and provide all of it. And yet, even as I was going through it, there was a moment when my mom told me, with a bit of surprise in her voice, that it felt like I was trying to adopt a baby. On the one hand, I agreed with her surprise. On the other, I knew that this dog was going to be so much more than just a cute puppy. I was training my medical equipment. I was signing on to have a dependent for over a decade. It wasn't all that surprising.

After the papers were signed and my bank account was made significantly lighter, I looked around, and my heart skipped because I hadn't really approached having things beforehand very well with Yaha. I had a crate and food, and... well, that was about it. I may have had a handful of treats, but I honestly don't remember very well. Suffice it to say, I was feeling very out-of-stock on whatever it was I needed. And that's never good.

On the flip side of the same coin, I didn't want to just go around spending money on things I didn't need yet--money that could be put toward Cor's training tuition.

Question: If you could tell someone going into this anything about stocking up on things ahead of time, what would it be?

From FIGZ: *Puppies are going to need a bit more than older dogs when they come into the house. You will go through a couple more stages, such as potty training, teething, fear periods, and adolescence. This may be the first time your dog has been away from its litter mates. Protecting your dog is your first priority.*

We like to set up a crate with an X-pen attached to form a sleeping area and a play area. When the puppy cannot be by your side or have your complete attention, the puppy should go to its play area. Our dogs love it because we give them a meaty bone while in there, so they do not see it as a punishment but rather as a reward, a great place.

TOYS; your dog needs many toys. Different shapes, different textures, different sounds. Dogs get bored. They like to change things up, or they may simply be going through a teething stage and want to chew on different toys. Some dogs prefer to chew on some toys while they like to snuggle with other toys. Having a variety to choose from will help prevent your table and chair legs, rugs, towels, curtains, power cords, etc., from becoming the next object of desire for a puppy to sink its teeth into. Be creative with toys. Don't underestimate the value of a good stick. Lots of chewing time, and it's free. Other great toys are empty water bottles, microfiber rags, and old socks tied together to form a rope.

Collar and leash. Start right away with the collar and leash. Yes, the puppy is not going to understand you want it to walk at heel with you, but they need to get used to wearing it. Let them drag the leash around with them. We recommend Lupine leashes as they are guaranteed for life, even if the puppy chews through them.

Grooming supplies. Different breeds require different levels of grooming and may require different shampoos than just the generic dog shampoo. Try to bathe the dog once a week to start. Make it a fun, relaxing, loving time. If a dog only gets a bath after rolling in the mud, it may start to see bath time as a punishment. Just FYI, some dogs love a good bubble bath.

From Amanda: This is something that people always want to ask me. The first thing is always a crate; that is always my number one. You want to crate train. It is so important for all of our service dogs to learn crate training because you don't know when you're ever going to need it, and you don't want them to freak out in a crate. So, the first thing: crates.

The next thing is food. Research the food that is best for your dog's health and best for your dog's breed. Every breed have different needs, so understanding that is very important. Dogs also require a lot of treats for training, so you're going to be spending a pretty penny on treats--start stocking up before you get the dog. Treats are a huge thing.

Other things you're going to need for your service dog in training are going to be chews and toys, which are huge. When you have a young dog, they have to chew. You cannot expect a young puppy not to chew. They're designed to relieve the teeth tension as they're growing and maturing, so those chews and toys are going to be a huge thing.

Beds are a big one for older dogs and not something I would suggest for young dogs inside their crate. Outside of their crate, it's fine; they love it. They might pee on it, so get something that's washable, but for your younger dogs, do not put beds in crates because they will probably shred it and eat something from it.

Other things for stocking up, obviously, your food bowl and water bowls--those are going to be important. Gear such as leashes and collars. If you plan on using any kind of head collar during training, it is highly suggested that you get it before you need it so that you can start working the dog and getting him used to it early on.

Then another thing that I usually suggest that people probably don't get as often is an X-pen. If you are working, busy, and not able to focus on your dog, they will have a play area, and you can provide a potty area in there. That way, they are able to continue potty training and have accidents in the correct place and not just all over your floor.

Question: What are things you see people assuming they need ahead of time that they either don't need or that are a waste of money in general?

From FIGZ: *Specialty treats. Starting a puppy with high-quality kibble or freeze-dried raw food works as a treat. Feed the puppy a small meal in the morning to help reduce the bile in its stomach, then feed the rest of the day's food as training treats throughout the day. This way, you will know the puppy is getting enough calories and enough training time.*

Companies do a great job marketing to humans. The colors added to dog food and treats are there for the human, not the dog. It looks pretty to us, so our dogs should want to eat it, so we buy it. Don't be fooled. You can give your dog human food. In fact, the dog may be healthier for it. Raw meat and bones, chicken or beef bone broth, sardines, salmon and salmon skins, blueberries, apples, cooked spinach, broccoli, carrots (frozen - our favorite teething toy), real cheese, peas, cauliflower, beans, rice, oatmeal. You may enjoy making your dog's food. Just be sure that you get a balanced recipe, so the dog gets all the needed vitamins and nutrients.

Remember, you are spending a lot of time, and possibly money, on getting this dog from puppy to service dog. You want the dog to live as long as possible with you. Eating healthy is the best way to ensure that.

From Amanda: *Honestly, if people want something comfortable in their dog's crate, I always suggest a primo pad first. That way, they have the cushion, they have the comfort, but it's a very easy-to-clean object. I really like primo pads because they provide the comfort and cushion that your dog needs. They are easy to clean, and they're not as easy to destroy. Love them for that reason. If they want a dog bed, use it outside of a crate.*

Other things that people think they need right away that they don't usually include a service dog in a training vest. If you're owner training and you think you need a vest right away, you're probably wrong. There are so many ways to socialize your dogs without having to go into public places nowadays that I highly suggest that first before you start taking your dogs into grocery stores or places like that.

2. Breeding Vs. Rescue

At this point, you've received the overview of your journey. You've got the map, even if you don't have the exact path, you need to draw on it. Now, you need the right partner--the puppy.

Just like if you were getting a pet dog, you have a few different ways this could go. You could go the breeder route or the rescue route. As you've seen, I've (tried to) go both. You've got a few pros and cons either way you go, but before I get into that, I want to make a point here.

Check with your trainer before taking me as the authority on this.

Your trainer knows what you're looking to train for.

Your trainer knows the best breeds and nuances you need.

Your trainer knows the dog world where you are.

ALWAYS defer to your trainer.

Okay, now that--hopefully--the bold print, italics, and underlining have helped those points sink in, here are the pros and cons I've seen in each option.

Breeder:

Cons:

--general prejudice

--long wait list

--higher price point

--lots of research to be sure you're not buying from a backyard breeder

Pros (when buying from a responsible breeder):

--You know the dog's pedigree

--You know any likely health challenges

--Sometimes, people buying a puppy to train as a service dog get bumped to the front of the list

--Quality, vital post-natal training, and socialization
--Responsible breeders know the breed they work with very intimately and try to preserve the core traits of that breed.

Rescue:
Cons:
--Don't know the medical history you're getting
--Don't know what previous training you're getting
--Don't know what fears you're getting
--If you need the dog to remain unaltered until a certain time, they don't always allow that. (Remember Teddy?)
--Shorter working life if you adopt an older dog.
--Potentially shorter working life, depending on unknown health issues.

Pros:
--Lower to nonexistent price
--Giving a dog a home that doesn't have one
--"Who rescued who" stickers
--Saving the one that saves you
- Giving another living being a purpose it otherwise may not have had the chance to have
--Arguably, the moral high ground
This decision can really only be made through personal preference AND a temperament test. It's also best to have your trainer sign off on the dog before you make any final choices. You don't want to get one and have the trainer have to tell you, "Okay, so chances are, this dog won't work out."
Remember the first dog I brought to the program--Ozzy?
When your trainer suggests against a dog...? Come close, it's a secret. Listen to them, friend! They don't want to have to drag you and an unfit dog through the program, both for their sanity--and yours--as well as for the sake of the dog.
That's what you have to be careful with, in a rescue dog. You don't know what you're getting. And while wanting to give a

home to a dog that doesn't have one is so honorable and valid--it's a valuable goal and one I can't praise highly enough--throwing a dog who isn't ready for this job into it is far more damaging than just letting the dog's true forever home come for it when the time is right. Beyond not knowing what array of temperaments and ages are in a rescue shelter for you to choose from, you don't know what you're getting in the realm of health and wellbeing backgrounds.

If you work with a dog for four out of the six to eight workable years in their life, and then you have to cut it short due to arthritis or other joint problems that they either got from their ancestry or wherever they were before they were with you, your time and money budgets are going to take even more of a blow than just training one dog. And, you're going to have to face the big baddie all service dog warriors and their human partners fear--what happens after they retire?--earlier than most. But that's something to cover at another time.

Along the same vein, you don't know what the puppy learned to fear before you got them. If they have a fear of cars, or escalators, or hard floors, and you don't find out until you're in the heat of the moment when you need them... well, I imagine you can figure out how that would go badly. *cringe*

...Then again, finding out strange things that your puppy is suddenly scared of for no apparent reason... well, anyone who's walked a puppy through a fear stage is no stranger to that moment. That moment of going, "...really? This? *shrug* well, if that's what we need to work through..."

It's really like playing a video game, almost--they give you more side quests than you could hope to finish to ensure you'll keep playing and not get bored with it. (And for those of you who didn't know that's what video games are doing... yeah, that's why they do that. You're welcome.)

There are cons to getting a puppy from a breeder, though, too. Not the smallest of which is the connotation those "the best breed is rescued" slogans have given the word "breeder."

No matter how much research you do into responsible breeders and the red and/or green flags to look for, there will always be someone who hasn't, and, if you're like me, you'll forever be able to feel the judgmental looks as the default setting if and when you admit to those who haven't done their research that (s)he's from a breeder. Although, on the flip side of that coin, there's this certain relief you get when you admit they are and the other starts asking questions that, while they don't say it outright, communicate, 'yeah, I understand; no need to apologize.' I honestly can't explain the strange relief those questions bring.

Also on that list of cons is... well, I think we can all admit that getting something of high quality just generally comes with a higher price tag. Dogs bred (especially by responsible breeders) are no exceptions, normally to the tune of a couple to several thousand dollars.

What do you get for that price? Many would say the dog-- that's it. However, that is simply not true. You are buying certainty in its ancestry (any responsible breeder will be able to give you the dog's predecessors to at least a few generations back and answer questions about the health history of those lines and why they bred these two dogs), its training (responsible breeders start getting the puppy used to new surroundings and textures and people from the moment they're born), and its future if you are unable to care for it (responsible breeders will always--ALWAYS--make it a condition of adoption that, should you die or become unable to keep the puppy, it come back to them.) The reason responsible breeders go through an interview process, and all the research into each line's histories--medical, job/show wise, and temperamental--is because responsible breeders take their job of continuing the breed *extremely* seriously. So the price is worth it, but definitely hefty.

Along with a hefty price and because responsible breeders don't overbreed, you run into a long wait list if you're buying a dog from a breeder. For this reason, if the breeder assures you something along the lines of, "Oh, we always have a litter ready for adoption," RUN AWAY! This means they are overbreeding their females--something extremely unhealthy for both the mamas and the babies. Responsible breeders generally only have two to three litters a year because of said overbreeding avoidance, and those two to three depend on how many intact females they have.

Question: If you could tell someone going into this anything about breeding vs rescues, what would it be?

From FIGZ: *Before breeding standard poodles for service dogs, both Tanya and Kerry volunteered in the training and caring for rescues. It wasn't until 2013 and 2014, after many rescues in their homes throughout their lives that they each bought and brought home their first purposely-bred poodle.*

Both rescue and purposely bred dogs can make phenomenal service dogs. Temperament, aptitude testing, training, and socializing are paramount to the success of every service dog. Unfortunately, we have found that around 80% of our rescues wash out due to the unknown. Unknown life traumas that ended them in a shelter, unknown birthing, rearing, and living conditions as puppies, unknown health issues of the parents, and the unknown temperament of the parents. With so many unknowns, your PTSD service dog may have PTSD themselves.

With an intentionally bred dog, we are starting with sound-temperament parents, who have been proven with conformation and sporting titles, and who have tested clear of all diseases available at that time. An added benefit of choosing a breeder who specifically breeds for service temperaments is knowing that the puppy has been raised from birth with service work as a priority. While we would love all of the puppies to be service dogs, we are lucky to get 3-4 out of 10. With our puppies, service dog training starts at 3 days old. Before the puppies can see or hear, we are already testing for scenting. Once eyes and ears have opened, we start the desensitizing process, getting them used to noises such as fireworks, crying babies, construction, household appliances, etc. Once they are around 4 weeks old we start socialization by bringing people over or taking puppies on field trips. Once the puppy is 7 weeks old, and after 3 evaluations, the service dog candidates are chosen.

From Amanda: *I want to start by saying I love my rescues. I ran a rescue for six years in Utah. I adored the behavioral part of it; I loved every bit of it, and I still love working with rescues. There is just something special about a dog who knows that they were trash at one point in their life and are just the light of your world the next. So, rescues, in my mind, have a special place in everyone's heart, and, honestly, they do have a place in service dog work for those who want to use them for the right reasons, and have an understanding of rescues. When you have this idea of working with a rescue, what you have to understand is that they're all going to come with behavioral problems. Every. single. rescue. does. and the biggest reason is that they were not raised or socialized how you wanted them to be up to the point that you got them. Whether that's an eight-week-old puppy, all the way through the three-year-old that we're looking at. So, anywhere in between, we have behavioral issues. And, also, genetics plays a giant role when it comes to a dog's mentality and the way dogs' adolescence, fear stages, and growth come. Rescues are a Russian roulette of a sort when it comes to genetic things and when it comes to behavioral things.*

When I talk about behavioral aspects in a rescue, I usually make sure people understand that the reason for the behavioral stuff is not because we're picking bad dogs; we still temperament test, we still get out there and we still make sure we are picking the best candidate we can find. It's easier to say yes to one from a breeder, because they're a clean slate and they've had the right socialization, while, with rescues, I have to be very picky. There are so many aspects when it comes to a service dog that we have to be picky. So, when I'm looking at my rescues, I go in and say no more often than I ever say yes. When I do get the yes, it doesn't mean that this dog is going to be amazing right away.

For example, I get a lot of rescues into our program because people can't afford a breeding prospect--and when you're working with a rescue, the best aspect of a rescue is the fact that they are cheaper. When I'm looking into my rescues and shelter dogs, what I see is not always what I get in a temperament test. What that means is, while the dog may have confidence out of the butt, and it is a very happy dog, excited to work with me, excited to do things, that's just a part of that dog's life. We can get into their home and go "Oh, this dog has a lot of work in the socialization department," because maybe it's nervous with other dogs--which we will test for, but we don't always see it. A temperament test is just a thirty-minute snapshot of the dog's life. So it's hard.

The other thing with rescues that a lot of people like, is the fact that the "adopt; don't shop" propaganda is very much out there. People feel bad for buying from a breeder; they feel like, if they buy from a breeder, they're killing a dog in a shelter. And it is so hard, again, for people like myself who came from the rescue world and have seen firsthand what that life is like to encourage people to go the breeder route. So what I usually like to tell people is that the dogs in rescues and shelters would make great pets--I mean, fabulous pets. But, if you want a service dog, and you want something that has a higher chance of not washing, a rescue usually is not going to be the place you're looking for. You're looking at a breeder more often than not.

Let's talk about breeding. I prefer this since I am a breeder, now. I got into the breeding world because of how many rescues washed out as service dogs and how many times I could not find what I needed from a rescue. I didn't leave the rescue world because I felt like it just wasn't my kind of world; I love my rescue dogs. I loved the behavioral aspect, and, as a behaviorist, it was amazing to work with those dogs, but, as a service dog trainer it is not what is needed for my program. So, we went the breeder route for many, many of our clients.

When you're looking at breeding dogs, the pros and cons of those are the facts that you do get a puppy to start with, and puppies are very malleable. They are a clean slate that you can start on the right foot. There is such a thing as a good dog from a breeder and a bad dog from a bad breeder. Just because you're going the breeder route does not mean you're going to get the perfect dog from any breeder out there. You have to find the right breeder. You have to make sure that you are going with someone who is health testing, who is socializing, who is raising these puppies correctly, and who is titling their adult dogs. Who is putting work into their breeding program? Breeding is not a money-making business, and if they're making money off of it, then they're doing it incorrectly.

When you're looking at the breeder route, the biggest pro is the fact that you get to find the breed that works best for you. And, not every breed is meant for every person. I am a golden retriever person. I adore the crap out of them, they are my breed, and my favorite thing, even though they like to annoy me at the same time. Now, I cannot handle Labrador retrievers. I know, they're just basically cousins to the goldens, but I can't stand them. I grew up with two of them; I love them. For other people. But, for me, it is golden or bust. And that is where the biggest pro for our clients comes in because we can find the right dog for the right person and the right temperament for the right person.

Another pro to getting a dog from a breeder is the fact that you have that genetic health background behind the animal. If you find the right lines, you will find the lines that have nice hips, nice elbows, and everything else that goes with it for that breed. Again, with goldens, we follow a very strict code of ethics, so I know that, genetically, my dogs' backgrounds have good eyes, they have good hearts, they have good indention, they have good patellas, and the hips and elbows, of course. And other things, in a genetic list that is beyond long. There is a lot of testing that goes into these dogs. So with that in mind, I know the history of my dogs' lineage, which is a very big plus for people looking at service dogs. You want a dog that's going to last you the dog's lifetime, not last you two years and then crap out.

Another pro with getting a dog from a breeder is male or female. While, yes, you could have an ideal gender when you're going with a rescue, you cannot go into a rescue and tell someone that you don't want certain traits but you do want other traits and you're like, "xyz" and have a long list of no-nos for your dog. Unfortunately, it does not work that way with rescues. You get what you get and you don't throw a fit because there's just no way of knowing what's coming up in a rescue, while with your breeders, you tell them the gender and the breed that you want and then you go and you temperament test and you find the best dog out of those requirements, and you do get a more personalized animal for your needs with the breeder route than you would with the rescue route, so that's a good thing for a lot of the breeding dogs.

Question: What, as someone deep in the dog world, are red/green flags for finding a breeder?

From FIGZ: *First and foremost select a breeder who understands how to breed, raise, and recognize a service dog candidate and what it takes to get that service dog candidate to the service dog finish line. If a breeder says all of their dogs could be a service dog they are lying, or at the least have no idea what they are talking about. If you are looking for a specific breed and the breeder you have found is not experienced enough in service dogs but is willing to work with you, make sure you employ someone who can help you select the right dog. It takes more than one evaluation at a single visit to pick the right dog. The dog cannot be selected at any age younger than 7 weeks of age as the Volhart and Advid dogs tests cannot give an accurate picture before then.*
Different breeds have different strengths and weaknesses. Within each breed, there are levels of energy and prey drive. When selecting a breeder, you need to know what the breed was

intended to do and compare if the dog's natural abilities line up with the service needed. This becomes a bit difficult when dealing with mixed breeds or dogs from a shelter because in some cases we don't know what the breed is and there is no guarantee that the dog will inherit one of the traits naturally occurring in one of the breeds mixed in the dog.

From Amanda: *The biggest thing you need to look for in a breeder is going to be the health testing aspect. When you are looking at health testing, every single breed has a different standard and code of ethics when it comes to testing your dog. You need to make sure that you are reading the breed standard according to the kennel club that you are following, which is AKC [American Kennel Club] here in America. You have to follow the breed standard and say, "What are all the testing requirements that are needed; let me make sure that my breeder has them all". All testing should be public knowledge. For instance, OFA, here in America, is the number one. If your dog comes from a breeder, their test results should be posted on OFA. And, they should be the full testing; not Prelims, not anything like that. You want to make sure health testing is done on your dog. If the breeder says 'We health test', and they don't provide verification, then they are lying.*

Now, I do have breeders I have talked to in the past that say, 'yeah, we health test; we take it to the vet all the time, and they checked them over and said they're healthy, and they have given them all their vaccines." That's not health testing. Health testing is hips, elbows, patellas, eyes, cardiac, genetic health testing--there's a whole list of things, every single breed is different, so you have to understand which breeds have which requirements. So, health testing is the number one thing. Then, when it comes to other red flags, I always ask why they bred the dogs they did. I, actually, usually don't even have to ask, I just look at the dogs, and I look at the titles. A dog doesn't need to be champion titled, per se, but you do want something on that dog to verify that, yeah, this dog is quality.

For instance, most of my dogs have titles on both ends: the front and the back. The front end is usually your championship titles, those are the titles that say "Yes, this dog meets breed standard," according to AKC, UKC, IABCA, or whatever club they got that title from, while the back end of the dog's name is all the fun titles, which could be your CGCs, all the way to dock diving titles, to anything. Those titles show that the dog has workability, which is going to be important when you're breeding for a service dog. You want an animal who can learn and work with its handler. If a dog can't do that, then you're going to run into problems. So you want workability in your lines.

Another thing that you look for with your breeders is how they raise their dogs. If they are raising them outside in kennels, you probably don't want a dog from that breeder. You want one that's highly socialized and very well-worked to become a service dog. You don't want them to be handled just every now and then and then be sent off to their homes to be worked. The socialization timeframe starts at four weeks of age. These breeders need to put the work in right away; you don't have the opportunity to do that; your breeder does.

Another red flag is going to be a breeder that makes you pick anything before seven weeks. If your breeder says "I need you to pick at two weeks of age," you're picking out of a lump of potatoes, and you don't know what is what. And breeders that do that, they don't care about confirmation, they don't care about temperament, and they don't care about genetic things. Your breeder needs to do the picking around the seven-week timeframe.

Lastly, you want a breeder that's willing to work with you. If you cannot get a good relationship with a breeder, you're not going to get a good dog. I mean, it is that simple. Your breeder should be your biggest cheerleader. These animals are your breeder's pride and joy. We don't breed them, send them off, and never care about them again. We adore these animals, we loved them first; we brought them into this world because of how much we love this breed, and we love these puppies; we love every single one of them. We want to be there for our puppies. The breeders who don't care about their puppies after they leave are usually the ones who are not doing it for the right reasons, and they're not going to be there to support you after anything happens, and that's not what you want. You want a breeder to be there with you side-by-side when it comes to anything regarding your puppy.

The last thing about a red flag for a breeder is going to cost, and it sucks because I have a lot of people who come to me saying, "I can't spend over xyz for a puppy," and in most cases, I refer them to a rescue, because every breed has a very standard set of costs. For instance, labs are pretty much around the one thousand to fifteen hundred dollar range, poodles are between fifteen hundred to two thousand, and golden retrievers are between twenty-five hundred to thirty-five hundred dollars. And there's a reason for each difference, and there's a reason for everything there, but it's not because golden people are trying to make more money, or labs don't make enough money, it's just that there are reasons. So, if you're looking at something in the four hundred to five hundred dollar range, you're probably getting a very crappy puppy.

Question: What, as someone deep in the dog world, are red/green flags for finding a rescue?

From Amanda: *I have seen crappy breeders and great breeders, just as much as I have seen crappy rescues and great rescues. Unfortunately, just because someone is a rescue, doesn't mean they're doing it right. You need to make sure that you are finding a rescue that's not just overfilling their home with all these shelter animals.*

I went onto a farm and found about forty animals just roaming on acres of land. They were just free roaming on this acreage. Some fights broke out while I was there, the animals were muddy and filthy, and instead of flea treatments, they put

DE everywhere, which is just not good for the dog's health or their lungs. You want a rescue that's probably working through foster systems, where there are people who take on one dog from the rescue, and keep it in their homework with it, play with it, raise it; it's in their home, and the rescue helps find it a home. Then, there are also shelters. Some shelters are just amazing and really do great at it and then there are others who, again, are overfilling.

The last thing with the rescues is that you want one that's going to be vetting your animals, spaying, and neutering them, or, if they're willing to work with you on holding off spaying and neutering, great, but that doesn't normally happen. You do want to work with rescues who are vetting the animals fully. Heartworm testing, the whole nine yards.

Do your research: this is a dog that's going to be medical equipment that you're going to be working with for years. You can't research your breeders or rescue too much. Your safety and health as well as your dog's depends on it.

Question: Why did you choose this? (purebred/rescue)

He chose us. --Rose family (rescue)

I believe a service dog is a medical device, and when saving and budgeting for one, took this and decided to go with what would have the least amount of risk involved (which I consider to be a purebred). --Leonard Duncan (purebred)

She was beautiful, I have a soft spot for white dogs, and she was sassy. I just love her personality. --Lauren Girsh (rescue)

Well, she chose me. I have the belief that your dog chooses you. --Kelsey (purebred)

I never exactly chose rescue vs purebred, I simply went with the first available dog that fit my needs. --Sam (rescue)

I was looking to start from scratch with a puppy and got my pick of the litter. --Anonymous (purebred)

When I went to meet Amanda and Scout's Legacy for the first time, they only had two dogs available, a German shepherd puppy, and Valor, who was a grown rescue. I worked with both for a little bit and, despite Valor's stubbornness, he and I were two peas in a pod and I decided he was the right one for me. --Janet (rescue)

I didn't. She was an accidental litter that my trainer took in. She was the only available older dog for me when I needed one. --River (rescue)

I had just lost my previous rescue (non-service dog) and I was at the shelter and I just wanted to play with puppies. Lo and behold, Roo and her sister were adorable. Roo (who was Cedar at the time) was more focused on me and generally just a goofball. I was walked through how to pick a service dog prospect, and Roo did a smidge better than her sister. I also had a preconceived idea about purebred dog breeders. Now that I have learned and experienced well-bred purebred dogs, I am open to either a rescue or purebred dog as my next service dog. --Kaleb Kelly (rescue)

I always had rescues in the past and they were great, but with Sugi, I wanted to stack the deck in my favor as much as possible, so I chose to go with a purebred, well-bred dog from a health-tested breeder and with a breed that tends to have a very good temperament for service work. I didn't care what breed my dog was, I just needed whatever would do the job best. --Marleigh (purebred)

3. Breed

In getting a dog from a breeder, you can choose your breed. If you get a rescue, you don't have the opportunity to choose. Is it really a big deal, though? How much influence can the breed of a dog have on the training and job ability?

More than you may think. Let me put it this way: if you are getting ready for a 5K relay race, who would you want on your team? Someone who has run twenty 5Ks in the last four years, or someone who has sat on the couch the entirety of those four years? You want the one better suited to the race, right? It's the same way for service dogs.

Question: If you could tell someone going into this anything about the importance/unimportance of breed in the training of a service dog, what would it be?

From FIGZ: *Temperament should always be considered the most important even before the breed. The best breed of dog with the wrong temperament will not make a good service dog.*

Before selecting a breed, the handler should make a list of all the things the service dog will need to do for them. Then rank the list in order of importance for each task. This now becomes your shopping list to find the best breed for you.

Each breed is different, having been bred for centuries for a different purpose or job, therefore, they will each be better at different tasks. A mobility dog needs to have a larger size, while a retrieval dog for a person in a wheelchair may need a smaller size to fit on the lap of the person in the chair. Some people have allergies and may need a hypoallergenic dog or a non-shedding dog. A PTSD dog needs a little bit of an attitude and a rock-solid demeanor. A diabetic alert dog needs a good nose but could be any size.

While any breed and mixed breed could be a service dog, it is best to select a breed that organically gives you behaviors that closely resemble the tasks needed. Appearance, color, and sex should be the least of the decision factors.

From Amanda: *Picking the right breed is everything for a service dog, because some breeds are just not meant to be service dogs for certain disabilities, and many, many groups of dogs are not meant to be service dogs for certain disabilities. For some reason, people see a German shepherd and think, "Oh, they're smart; it's going to be easy to train," and the problem with that is the fact that German shepherds have high anxiety about the job at hand. They're supposed to be a working dogs, and when you take a dog who is meant to have high-drive working abilities, it's going to have anxiety. Now, the anxiety inside of that animal is a good thing, for the jobs they are bred to do; it is not a good thing for a service dog for a psychiatric person.*

The same aspect could go for a livestock guardian breed, or any guardian breed, for instance. So, if the dog is meant to guard something, and be a protector, it is not going to be a good candidate for someone who cannot control that animal. Again, psychiatric people do not do well with guardian breeds. Seizure-response dogs are not good for guardian breeds. These breeds need someone who is going to be in control at all times. Not a handler who can't keep their control and mentality around the dog at all times, because if the dog thinks you're in trouble, it's going to go into protection mode, it's not going to go into "I need to help you," mode.

Instincts are everything. Every dog breed was bred with certain temperaments and certain instincts and certain workabilities. That is why we have so many different breeds--we didn't create thousands of breeds just for us to have the same dog all over the place. We need to remember that as the human race, these are all animals that were created for a certain purpose.

Golden retrievers are duck-hunting dogs. They were not created just to be family pets. Now, they were created to have the temperament to be a family pet and to go and be duck-hunting dogs. You have to look at the history of this breed--where did it come from? Where did it originate? Why were they created? And if you see that there are creations in this breed that probably don't fit a service dog lifestyle, you probably don't need that dog as your first service dog.

With the genetic component of every animal, research is a huge thing. On top of genetics, you also have to look at the size of an animal, because, if you're working with mobility dogs, you can't get a small little Papillon to do the job that you need--you have to find the right size and ratio for your disability. Giant breeds are needed in the service dog world for the right size and ratio. But, you have to look at the temperament to see if you can live with that temperament, that size, and ratio. Then, you have the aspects of male/female, because, even though breeds play a big role, gender does also. I did mention in the breeding area that breed is a huge deal because temperament is going to be the number one in how they can handle themselves, so a good example are the three service dog breeds out there that are just the best quality for most people.

One is golden retrievers; they're happy-go-lucky. They also have hard fear stages.

Two are Labrador retrievers. They are crazy until three, but they have nice fear stages where they don't get scared as easily as goldens.

The third one is poodles. They are happy-go-lucky. They do have hard fear stages, but not as hard as goldens. The hardest part about a poodle is the fact that they have to be groomed so much more often.

Every dog in those three categories has a pro and a con, and you have to figure out which con is easier to live with for you.

You see, through the ages, humans have bred dogs. In the "old days"--just a mere couple hundred years ago--we bred them for specific jobs. Collies for herding, schnauzers for hunting small vermin, rottweilers for herding larger animals such as cattle (one of the reasons they have such a high pain tolerance), and poodles for hunting waterfowl and the like (yes, really). These days, breeding is more often done for the look of the dog--with a handful of exceptions. We have the breeds we do for a reason, and they still look to fulfill their ancestral duties and jobs.

Modern humans have found ways to make those ancestral duties work for modern-day needs. While you may not need a rottweiler to herd cattle--although some people undoubtedly still do--people have made use of their resultantly high pain tolerance to give them the name "nanny dogs." These dogs, if trained right, are some of the best dogs around children because of their pain tolerance. They can put up with the ear-tugging and tail-grabbing. They can handle the rough-and-tumble-ness of kids. And that herding tendency hasn't left them either.

Dogs of those ancestrally herding or hunting breeds tend to be more aware of where their humans are. Of course, this comes with a higher tendency for nipping or ankle-biting, as it were. Herding tendencies.

I say this all as someone who, admittedly, hasn't owned a rottweiler. I have, however, owned two lab mixes, and, yeah. Herding tendencies.

All that to say, it is out of these ancestral duties that we get, in the service dog world, what are called the "fab four"--labs, goldens, poodles, and smooth collies, This refers to the best four breeds for a service dog. These fab four dogs are the four that are best suited, on the whole, to be service dogs. Of course, there are unicorns in every breed, and some people can train other breeds to be very good service dogs, but you can't count on finding that elusive unicorn, and the people I know who can train other breeds have either a lot of help or have been doing it for a while.

This is where going the rescue route, and hoping to find that one-in-a-million puppy can get you into trouble; hence why the 'fab four' is an important distinction. Also why listening to your trainer is vitally important. Let me say that again: listening to your trainer is vitally important. At least, if you want to get through this as painlessly as possible.

Now, there are exceptions to every rule. Take Yaha, for example. Half of Yaha was part of the fab four. However, the other half of him wasn't; it was a German shepherd. And that came through--what his ancestors had been trained for. Protection and guarding as well as herding.

I know many people will argue that breed only gets you so far, and, in a way, they're right. As I said, there are unicorns in every breed. But, just like you don't want to shove a mechanic into the operating room to perform open-heart surgery without some training in... well, open-heart surgery, you don't want to put a dog that's not fit for service dog training into a service dog program.

Just like the mechanic has worked with machinery before and knows the principles of how each piece and cog impacts the others--and that the body works loosely the same way--a dog is a dog. However, just like how an electric circuit or the engine of a car doesn't translate nicely to open-heart surgery, a dog that isn't suited for a specific job is more of a hindrance than a help.

Don't hear what I'm not saying. These are not the "best dogs". I am in NO WAY saying that other dogs are useless or a moot point or anything like that. However, a corgi cannot match a Belgian malinois's jumping capabilities (look it up; they're unreal), a poodle can't match a rottweiler's pain tolerance, and a Saint Bernard can't match a lab's or Dalmatian's endurance. Specific breeds just tend to have a natural bent for specific abilities. And, when you have a specific job for a dog to perform, you need to set yourself up for success as much as possible; for service dogs, the fab four are it.

(Someone I know who has been in the service dog world for a long time is rather adamantly training Pyrenean mastiffs, and she's doing well--remarkably so for such a stubborn breed--but I again refer to the "have been doing it for a while." A best practice is to not stray very far outside the fab four for your first service dog in training.)

Question: What breeds are best for which jobs?

From Amanda: *When it comes to breeds, you have to look at it again from the temperament aspect of each client. A lab is great for almost any job, they are. But the problem is a lab is not great for most people, because they're just too high energy, they're too high strung, and they're just too much dog for most of your first-time handlers. This is a very hard question because it's not just about the job itself, it is about the person who is handling the dog.*

Your top four breeds are your labrador retriever, golden retriever, standard poodle, and smooth collie. Smooth collies are harder to come by, though, and they're not as easy to get the right temperament, so I always steer clear of smooth collies. I just do. I would emphasize to the people reading this that it is about them just as much as it is about the dog. While there is the fab four, people need to understand how to live with the pros and cons of those fab four.

Those who get German shepherds, for instance, generally struggle three times more with their dogs than any of my golden people. Lab people and German shepherd people usually struggle the same. My German shepherd handlers struggle so much more than any golden retriever person out there. And that's because goldens have it in their mindset to do whatever their handler wants, while shepherds have it in their mindset to problem-solve. And that can sometimes be a problem for first-time handlers.

Now, there is a reason why people don't suggest shepherds, malinoises, Duchies, border collies, Australian shepherds, or anything like that to newbies. Because, when the dog is smarter than you, you're going to run into problems. And, yeah, these dogs are smarter than most of their people. They're not great for that reason. They're also not great because of the anxiety aspect; a lot of people get service dogs these days for anxiety. So, they're not going to be great for those handlers, and then, they're just too much dog for most people. They require more work because they need an outlet; so, for instance, my German shepherd does three other dog sports on top of her service dog work to keep her happy and healthy--mentally as much as physically.

Beyond ^this^, which breed you choose will largely swing in the direction it will, due to personal preference on a few things.

1. Grooming.

Poodles take a heck of a lot of grooming.

Labs, not so much.

Collies and goldens fall in the middle.

With Yaha, grooming amounted to, basically:

- a bath every couple of weeks
- brushing him out every few days
- keeping his nails trimmed

Cor... has a lot more to it than that. As a point of interest, here's a 10,000-foot-view list:

- bathe as close to every week as possible
- blow dry (yes, really)
- cut hair, anywhere from every week to every four
- pluck ear hair (yes, really)
- trim nails
- brush as needed (the longer there is between haircuts, the closer to every day this falls).

A little bit more, yeah? I could go more in-depth, but that's not the point here.

With that increase in grooming (3-5 hours per every week or two if you do it all at once), you gain a little something in their being as non-allergy-inducing as a dog can be. ...well, non-hairless dogs, anyway. Poodles also don't shed, and their hair is closer to human hair than most dogs' fur, meaning their dander is different than most dogs', which is why poodles are largely considered the most hypoallergenic dogs. This, therefore, minimizes the need for vacuuming as often due to a canine presence.

This was a big plus for our family and heavily weighed the scales in favor of a poodle.

2. Speaking of shedding, that's an aspect to think of, as well. All dogs with fur (save poodles and any doodle mixes lucky enough to have inherited their poodle parent's hair-not-fur coat-- not something that is guaranteed, interestingly enough) blow their coats.

I've seen people with goldens specifically who will get up after the group training and leave behind a veritable blanket of fur when they're blowing coat. This is why it is so important to brush them out when they're shedding. As I mentioned before, you also get to pick up the fur (likely through vacuuming). Brushing regularly won't stop them from shedding, but it will minimize the thickness of the said blanket.

3. They differ in regard to how eager they are to please their people. Goldens are at the far end of the spectrum in that it seems to be their one goal in life, with labs close behind and poodles generally taking up the rear as a bit more stubborn. They're by no means on the opposite end of the spectrum, just a bit closer to the apathetic middle.

4. Something else you'll want to consider is how heavy of a puppyhood you're willing to deal with.

Labs' puppy hoods are... rough (I've heard it said a lab's puppyhood is the hell of the fab four's puppyhood. I'm not claiming that, exactly, but it is rough. Tip: get them to see that sticks and antlers and bones are their designated chews. It won't happen overnight, but if you keep directing them to those when they start gnawing, you'll save your furniture, remotes, shoes, socks, various home electronics, etc). Like with a lot in life, things balance out in this way; though a lab's puppyhood is, in general, easily the worst of the lot, when they mature they are some of the sweetest dogs you'll ever meet.

Goldens and poodles generally have a much easier puppyhood. It's still not as adorable as they are--far from it--but it's easier. Teething isn't as hard, particularly.

A golden's easy-to-please mentality also makes it quite a bit easier. This leads to our next point rather nicely.

5. Something that can help with a poodle's puppyhood--and one of the reasons I chose a poodle--is that poodles are smart. In a puppy, this can help, but it can also be tricky because they learn fast, and if you don't give them something to learn--if you don't work their minds--they will teach themselves. Most of the time, if this is the case, they'll teach themselves things you'd rather they not learn. However, if you focus heavily on training as a puppy--particularly decency training/doggy etiquette, this can be invaluable. If you're able to lay some ground rules before the adolescent stages kick in and keep with it, things--theoretically--go much better.

I am not saying that the other breeds aren't smart. Each of the fab four is on the high end of doggy intelligence, teachability, and a cooperative spirit, because, in a service dog, these are very valuable traits. They learn fast, and they can think for themselves. Service dogs, like police dogs, sled dogs, or any other working dog, need to know when to disobey.

Say a handler told a seeing eye dog to cross the street, but the dog sees a truck coming that their handler doesn't hear. They need to know to disobey the order to cross the street. If a dog is told to go to the car, but can tell their human has a seizure, critical diabetes situation, or the like, coming up, they need to be able to measure which is more urgent. Poodles are on the high, high end of doggy intelligence.

6. Energy level.

This one doesn't differ breed by breed as much as it differs from dog to dog. However, the breed can have a definite influence.

You have four landings, with a staircase between each, as it were.

--Low energy
--Medium energy
--High energy
--Very high energy

Cor is low energy, Yaha was high energy, and Ozzy was very high energy the first day we had him, settling down on the staircase between medium and high after the nervous "new place!" energy fell off toward the end.

With low energy, you don't have to put forth much effort into wearing the dog out. Cor and I get up in the morning, I let him out, feed him, and play with him for about an hour before going back into my hermit cave bedroom, where I work for a couple of hours until I come out for lunch, and he wanders around, chewing on a stick or antler, or maybe playing with a toy. After this I go back into my room, and he's pretty much good until any time from 2:30-4, and then he's up until about 6:30-7, when he falls asleep on the living room floor, having had dinner between 5:15-5:30. There are days, though, when Cor fancies himself a social... what's a stronger word than a butterfly? leading to a necessary walk or ride.

Yaha... well, I was lucky to get any work in before bedtime at 8:30. On the early end.

The first day we had Ozzy, we spent most of the day outside playing fetch and going for walks. On the second day, he took a nap in the middle of the day for a couple of hours.

I cannot tell you how thankful I was to learn that Cor was as low energy as he is--I cannot keep up with the kind of dog my aunt and uncle can. (They're all kinds of outdoorsy; rock climbing, hiking, camping, you name it.) I'm a bit partial to my downtimes when I can write or read or do any of the other ten things I do on the side.

So, while I loved Yaha, the fact that he had as much energy as he did and needed to go on as long of walks as he did (45 minutes each morning, give or take 15), wasn't the best situation for me.

That's the big thing--you need to find a dog you can work with. You don't want to have a dog you need to work around-- pinching this, pulling that, waking up this much earlier to fit the walk in before he can go in the kennel so you can go to church.

You'll have some of that no matter what dog you get--you're trying to make at least two schedules align--but you don't want every day to be that.

The above differences are why the fact that FIGZ is on call for their dogs' entire lives for their clients to reach out with questions is so valuable to me. Breeders have extremely intimate knowledge of their chosen breed. Amanda trains the dogs individually, and breeds goldens, so she knows the dogs individually and goldens as a breed, but because FIGZ breeds poodles and knows them so intimately, I can ask them questions about poodles in particular, to make sure I get advice due to both his breed and his unique personality and the service dog training program.

Question: As someone very deep in the dog world on the whole, can you share your thoughts on dogs' energy levels?

From Amanda: *Your service dog's energy levels are something you need to research before you get into the service dog world and before you get a dog. Because every single breed has a different energy level that is required in their temperament. If you are looking at a breed--for instance, a German shepherd--and you are saying "I want to get a German Shepherd because they are smart, and they learn quickly," but you don't research enough to understand that German shepherds need a lot of physical and mental outlets to be able to be happy, it won't end well. German shepherds do not do well as just service dogs; they do best as service dogs, sport dogs, and extra things. They are not a one-time, "I go out in public once in a blue moon and work," they are an "I need to get out and work as often as I possibly can," kind of dog. So, in that sense, someone with a low energy level would not fare well with a German shepherd. Someone with a high disability would not fare well with a German shepherd. It's something that I'm always stressing to people--if you are not ready to do three times more work, then you should not get a German* shepherd. They just do better when they can do a sport on top of being a service dog--dock diving, barn hunting, rally, obedience, all of those are something where the dog has an outlet, and it's not just having to focus on you and your disabilities. So temperament and energy levels are huge things when looking at dogs.

The same can be said for a Pyrenean mastiff; we have a couple of those in the program. Pyrenean mastiffs, they are the opposite of German shepherds. They have lower energy levels; they sleep about seventy percent of the day because they conserve energy. Pyrenean mastiffs were bred to protect their land, so they needed to be able to move quick, move fast, be brute, but also have the energy to do it. If they were just running around playing all day they couldn't do their job. They are on the lazier spectrum. But that wouldn't work well for someone who wants to go biking, hiking, or doing things often, because their dogs can't keep up with them.

Some people with disabilities are still very active, so if you're an active person, you have to find the right dog for you. Labs usually fit well with active people, because they're very active also.

Now, here's the catch-22 with energy levels. You need to make sure you have a dog who has an amazing amount of energy to be able to withstand going out and working that seven to an eight-hour day, if they need to, but you need to see if that dog can also shut down and just chill for twelve hours in the day, because of your disability. So the right breed has to play a role in all of this--you need to have an on/off kind of dog. And so, service dogs need energy to do their job, but you don't need an excessive amount of energy, and you don't want too little energy. Finding the right breed with the right amount of energy as a puppy will usually help. But the biggest catch is puppies are still puppies--they are going to have more energy at six months old than they ever would at three years old. Patience is a virtue.

Question: Every breed has unique challenges and benefits. If someone were going to get the same kind of dog you have, what are some words of wisdom you would give them before they get started?

You need lots of patience and to be prepared for the hard-headed beast. --Rose family [pit bull mix]

Be prepared for high physical and mental stimulation needs! Very early on, this made things difficult for me due to my physical disabilities. --Leonard Duncan [standard poodle]

Have patience and lots of it. Be stern, and consistent--no wiggle room; don't slack. --Lauren Girsh [heeler/husky mix]

Be more interactive when they are little; get out, go on walks, handle their hyperness, and control them to where they understand that they have to calm down and can't get into things. Those are the two biggest issues I have with mine. It's her wanting to get into my daughter's toys and constantly bark when she's not near me, or she's just being too hyper. Get them out and get them into something interactive and fun to where it keeps their mind busy and they are less hyper. --Kelsey [labrador]

Be prepared for a power chewer. Nothing in your house will be safe! :) --Sam [pit bull mix]

Teach them to poop in one spot! Cavaliers are notorious for "poop walking." haha --Anonymous [Cavalier King Charles Spaniel]

Firstly, don't get a hound breed. Secondly, if you do get a hound, work on impulse control regarding prey animals like rabbits and squirrels. --Janet [redbone coonhound mix]

Don't. Don't get this breed unless you can deal with problems when they aren't feeling up to working or doing anything, and they misbehave. They are not a good dog for beginners (as a beginner) and, also, don't breed mutts up. --River [labrador, mastiff, rottweiler mix]

Don't. Kidding. Be prepared for attitude. From the dog, from the public, and from family. --Kaleb Kelly [american pit bull terrier/Staffordshire terrier mix]

I always warn new poodle parents about the grooming involved and what it'll cost and that you can learn to do it yourself, but it isn't as easy as it seems. I explain the importance of starting grooming early, and keeping whatever haircut you can maintain. There's no shame in keeping your dog super short if that's all you're able to handle. --Marleigh [standard poodle]

One little-known fact is that standard poodles are like Dobermans. They are about the same size and structure. They train the same way and they protect the same way. A standard poodle is not just a big ball of fluffy cuteness, these guys go hard-core. There is nothing dainty about a standard poodle. Adolescence can be quite challenging, especially for a male. As they start to mature they will naturally move from servicing you to trying to protect you. This will be a time when a trainer on call is useful and you will learn to find a lot of inner strength. This is usually the time a male will wash out of a program. –Tanya Figliozzi [standard poodle]

4. Temperament

One of the most important things in a service-dog-in-training candidate is temperament.

Temperament is, at its most basic, several different aspects of the dog, for example, the temper, social ability, focus, teachability, problem-solving, and natural attitude, all looked at as one cohesive trait of the dog.

This is important because a dog that will snap at the slightest provocation or be distracted by everything to the point that it will never focus on its handler will not be a good service dog. That would be a dog that is more dangerous to take out in public than it is helpful--no matter how many tasks it knows. And taking a dangerous dog out in public will not make you friends with anyone.

You also don't want a dog that doesn't want to learn, or, when presented with something new, doesn't try to figure it out, or gets frustrated. That, too, is dangerous. For example: if a guide dog is in the middle of the store, trying to get their person out of the building, and there is a large pallet of boxes blocking their path, you want the dog to be able and willing to problem solve. You don't want the dog to just kind of go, "Well, that's it. We're stuck here, now. Sorry, Human." Or, if a seizure response dog's person's seizure looks different from one day to the next, you want a dog that can look at the situation and go, "Well, if I normally do A when something similar to this happens, I should probably do A now," rather than not paying attention because it looks a bit different, or getting frustrated because it doesn't know what to do.

This is how we get stories of a guide dog in the twin towers during 9/11 that led multiple people out of the building because part of its training is finding a clear path to the door. It's how we get stories of a hearing dog that was able to warn its person that something was wrong with the bus they were on, consequently rescuing everyone from a bus no one else was aware was on fire. You want a smart dog that's able to think for itself and figure things out, without being so overwhelmingly stubborn that it decides some days to just not do the thing, and you cannot sway it.

Are these traits they're born with?

...kind of.

They aren't born knowing how to do it, by any means, but there are signs that puppies can give those who know how to look for them as to whether they're worth taking a shot on.

From Amanda: *There's been a lot of research into [temperament]. Temperament is just as much a genetic trait as it is an environmental trait. You can take a dog with a genetically good temperament and ruin it. You can also take a dog with a genetically bad temperament and never make it better because genetics play a big role when it comes to the way a dog thinks and a dog responds to scenarios. Some breeds are prone to fear stages that are harder than others, some breeds are prone to dog aggression, human aggression, and other issues. You have to understand that genetics is just as important when it comes to temperament as it is with how you raise them. Pick the breeds that best fit the temperament that you need for the job at hand.*

This is why temperament testing is crucial in choosing a service dog, because, if you choose and adopt, or buy your dog before getting it temperament tested, and it turns out that you didn't see a red flag in your first meeting with the dog, or misread something in their body language, or didn't get the dog around something that, had you, would've given you a huge red flag, you're now in a very stuck position.

Question: Who should temperament test a dog/puppy? When? Where? What is the importance of that person doing the temperament testing as opposed to someone else?

From Amanda: *It should be the trainer, and it should not be the person getting the dog. So, for instance, I usually don't temperament test my dogs, if I can help it. We didn't get lucky enough, because of COVID this year, to temperament test our litters with someone else, but, usually, you want someone else; not the person who raised the dogs. That's the first thing. Seven weeks and on is when we do it. You usually want to find a place that is not a room that the dog is used to being in, so you want a new room. With puppies, that can be just a bedroom, or--with adult dogs--Lowes, or something like that.*

The importance of trainer temperament testing is that we are looking for the subtle cues that dogs give in their body language to determine if the dog has what it takes to become a service dog. While most people just see a happy-go-lucky dog, we see a dog with whale eyes, panting, pacing, anything that just says, "Hey, this dog is very nervous, not excited to be here." And then, again, have it be someone that's not the handler, even if the handler is a trainer. We love to see the good in our dogs, we don't like to point out the bad traits, so having someone else do it gives you that third-person point of view, which is very important.

From FIGZ: *A temperament test is a snapshot in time. It is important to take many snapshots so a full picture of the dog can be formed. On day 1, we are taking a snapshot of the puppies' conformation. From 3-16 days old, we are taking snapshots of scent work in the puppies. At 5 weeks we do the first mini-Volhard test. At 6 weeks we have a puppy party; invite past, present, and future puppy owners, and evaluate how the puppies act in a new space with new people asking them to do new things. At 7 weeks we do our final snapshot. These are the Volhard and Avid dog tests.*

In a place the puppies have never been, the test is performed by a person the puppies have never met, who understands how to bring out the true nature of our breed. We use a collaboration of all the tests to select our service dog candidates and determine what type of service each candidate would best excel.

5. Socialization

Speaking of being in a very stuck position if you don't do something and/or listen to your trainer, socialization can be a make-it-or-break-it time for a puppy. It is vital to get this in during the first sixteen weeks of their life.

If you are buying a puppy from a responsible breeder, they will have already started the socialization process with your puppy. During the first sixteen weeks, your goal is to get them out and around as many new and exciting places, animals, people, sounds, etc. as you possibly can. It doesn't have to be long--even a five to ten-minute outing is tiring for a puppy as they take in all the new sights and sounds of the place.

Note: during these weeks is also when you are in the process of getting them their shots. Until they have had all their shots, their feet can't touch the ground in public, so you'll get to carry them everywhere. (Unless they're a poodle puppy that *jumps out of the shopping cart when your back is turned*.)

In these first sixteen weeks of a puppy's life, its brain is in a place it will never be again. They take in what their senses tell them like a sponge, just accepting it as part of the world. After those sixteen weeks, the chemistry in their brain changes as they grow and go into their first fear stage, which is a bit more mild. During these sixteen weeks, they are going through socialization. After those weeks, it's all desensitization.

This is where the generation my trainer calls "pandemic puppies" is at a bit of a disadvantage. Take Cor, for example. For the first ten weeks of his life, he was shown new and strange surroundings and textures and animals. Part of that was taking him into public. I carried him around Home Depot and Hobby Lobby and various other places the first week I had him. (Not pet stores, though, as you don't know what diseases may be floating in the air that your puppy hasn't gotten his shots for.) A week after we got him, quarantines and shutdowns became the new normal. During this time of his life, then, when it was *imperative* that he get out in public and be around strangers, it also became *imperative* that we not go out in public. See the problem?

This is where you need to get creative with outings, then. Because, maybe, for you, it's not quarantine. Maybe it's a vehicle that's getting repaired for an inordinately long time (we've had that, too!), or you become sick or break a leg and can't go out and walk them around. There could be any number of reasons that you can't just go walk around Hobby Lobby or Home Depot or Lowes or whatever.

So how do you handle this? A few of the ways we did it were:

--Obstacle courses in the backyard experimenting with different textures and skills. For example:

*run across a bathmat

*sit in a kiddie pool

*walk under a chair

*go over a broomstick

*walk across a wobble board (a piece of wood on top of something to make it unsteady)

--If someone you know is driving to a store or post office or somewhere like that, go along, and just sit in the car with the door open. (Keep the puppy on a leash!) If your puppy has had their shots, let them walk around outside while you stay in the car. Otherwise, just watch the world go by.

--Talk to those you know with older dogs who have had all their shots. Arrange a short puppy play date if you can.

--Go for a walk along a different path than normal

--Introduce the puppy to something they wouldn't see in the normal course of the day--something in the basement or attic, maybe, (be careful! Puppies are babies and don't know what things can hurt them!) let them explore the tub.

--Go for car rides and let them sit on your lap to look out the window and/or crack a window so they can smell outside.

--Listen to loud music

--Sit out front with them on the leash and let them watch, smell, and hear the cars and people go by.

--Ask a friend to take their dog out front of their house and walk your puppy by. If they're able to put their feet on the ground, have them obey a few simple commands with the dog serving as a distraction.

The biggest part of this is remembering that 'socialization' doesn't have to be big; it just has to get the puppy around new and strange things they can explore or learn to ignore. As a puppy, anything new is big.

Question: If you could tell someone going into this anything about socialization, what would it be?

From FIGZ: *Socialization is one of the most important things you will do with your dog. We start socializing our puppies as soon as Mom allows visitors. Our puppies go back and forth between our homes to get exposure to different sounds, family members, and routines. We take them on multiple field trips. Past puppies have gone to a horse ranch, brewery, the mall, and a Christmas festival.*

Socialization during the first 16 weeks is crucial but must be done carefully due to the puppies' lack of immunity to diseases such as parvo, and distemper. Anything you want your adult service dog to do should be experienced as a puppy. To experience something the puppy only needs to see, not necessarily touch. Puppies should be taken out and carried in your arms, in a basket, or in a stroller. The puppy needs to see all different shapes, sizes, ages, and colors of people; some with facial hair, sunglasses, hats, piercings, and tattoos. As for animals, puppies should see birds, fish, rodents, goats, cows, cats, and other dogs. The puppy must meet large and small dogs, different colored and spotted dogs, dogs with pointy ears, dogs with scrunchy faces, dogs who are dyed different colors, dogs with floppy ears, and dogs whose teeth stick out.

Proper socialization will help ensure that the puppy will have a better transition through fear periods and new situations.

From Amanda: *Socialization is such a big task at hand. There is a very short time frame in a dog's life that is the socialization time frame, and you have to understand that once you are out of that time frame, you are no longer socializing your dog, you are desensitizing. There is a difference between those two words.*

Socialization happens around the four-week mark of a dog's life to twelve to sixteen weeks, depending on the dog. Most end around twelve weeks, some can go longer, up to sixteen weeks, but, again, most of the time the socialization time frame is done at twelve weeks.

Socialization in itself is a word that best describes a time frame in a dog's life where their brain is a sponge, and they take in a new scenario and they say, "This is how my life just is," and they go with it. They're not scared of it. During this time frame, the socialization period is a great way of teaching your puppy that these new things that are happening in its life are okay and good.

After that twelve to sixteen-week timeframe, you are no longer teaching your puppy that these things are good; you are showing it that they're not going to die from these scenarios, so you're desensitizing them. Their brains are no longer a sponge; their brains stop taking in these new scenarios and saying, "I'm okay with it," and start turning it into, "Am I going to live or die from this scenario?"

Because you're out of the socialization time frame early on, you need to make sure that you are getting that dog worked and socialized right away; these dogs need to get out. They are not meant to be at home, so, as service dogs in training, we get our puppies out to different environments as much as possible. I don't need a vest for these timeframes, but we do get them out. We get them worked, we get them to see new people, new animals, and new scenarios, and we do it safely. Yes, Parvo and other illnesses are a fear, because they're not fully vaccinated, but the biggest fear of any service dog's career is the fact that they wash due to fear issues. And if you are not getting that puppy out before the sixteen weeks time frame, you have now lost your chances at socializing, and you are going to have an uphill battle with a fearful animal.

You need to make it fun. It's not just about going out and throwing them to the wolves, it is about going out and having fun. So, when you go to that new store, you're bringing those fun treats, you're bringing those good times, you're bringing their toys, and you're just playing with them. You're not going out to work; you're not going out to do: sit, down, stand, stay, heel, leave it, watch me, all that fun stuff that we are going to be working on. Those outings should be meant to be enjoyable. What you're teaching your puppy at this age is that, while, yes, we can work on some things while we're out, the biggest thing that they're working on is seeing the world around them. That, in itself, is more important before the four-month mark than all the training that can happen at any time in this dog's life.

When people get new puppies, I always tell them that you need to be ready to work hard for a good long while. When you get this new puppy, the first thing you do is you start taking it out, and you start working it and you start making it see new environments immediately. If you are not prepared to get a puppy and start going places with it, then you are not prepared to owner-train a service dog yet. You have to wait for the right time in your life. It is okay to say no to a dog until you are ready for it.

A puppy should be going out anywhere between three to four times a week--it really should. And it's not like you're going out for hours on end; you are going out for twenty minutes to a new place. And sometimes that drive is going to take you longer than the outing itself.

During the socialization timeframe, you have to be prepared to go to new places. Someone else's home is a new place. Going to Cabela's is a new place. Sometimes you go to the same place twice just because you can experience something new both times. The more you do with your puppy before they're four months of age, the better they get, and the less fear issues you're going to be running into.

6. Behavior Issues

This early age--and all of the service doghood--isn't easy for a dog. With all the smells and sights and sounds around it's hard to stay well behaved.

How long can you stay "behaved" in a day without a break? I know, for me, it's not easy. People are draining. Some more than others, but all humans are draining. The more rigid and strictly "polite" I have to be, the harder it is. I can say things around my family that I would never say to others. If my sisters ask for a pencil and I respond with something along the lines of, "Absolutely not; how could you ask so much of me?" It normally ends in laughter and them using said pencil. If I responded that way to an acquaintance or business relationship, it'd likely end in anger or hurt. There have been a couple of times when any one of us would say, "I love the dog more than you," when that isn't true. We're able to say it because we know the other knows the truth. The other is a safe place that won't take everything we say at face value.

When your dog acts out or tests boundaries, it's like that. They know they can trust you and that you will not stop loving them because they act out. Of course, in the vest, this needs to be corrected. They need to learn that acting like that isn't acceptable on the job even though it's forgivable at home. But, at home, you can't expect them to constantly be on their best behavior.

These dogs have accidentally scratched me or stepped on my full bladder more than anyone would hope. You can't blow up or become mad every time they mess up. Does that mean you should just let them chomp away on your leg until you can see the bone? Absolutely not. But there needs to be a middle ground--discipline and correction without anger. With grace.

With forgiveness as they try to figure out what life with a human constitutes.

It is your job to help them with this. That takes understanding and patience. Take a good, long look at yourself and see if you're able to offer that. If not, you may need to reconsider how you're going to approach this path, because dogs are very perceptive to human moods and voice tones. If you're feeling frustrated or angry, they can hear that, just like they can hear your happiness and excitement. They can feel your worry and fear. They can feel your emotions with a little more accuracy than a lie detector. What this means is, when you're frustrated and they continue doing what they're doing--which will happen--they may simply be trying to see how far they can push you. This is when you need to be firm, without getting angry or overly emotional.

You shouldn't yell at them, you shouldn't chase them. You need to pull out the mom/dad voice. You know the one--where you realize that they mean what they're saying, and this is your last warning, even if they don't outright say that.

Good discipline doesn't constitute hitting or kicking or otherwise throwing one's weight around. It constitutes setting boundaries and allowing there to be consequences that don't harm the other being when those boundaries are broken. That's what these puppies will need.

7. Fear and Adolescent Stages

Most of these behavioral issues will happen in what is called an adolescent stage, which is exactly what it sounds like. Y'all know the difference between a sweet little baby that just wants to be carried around and the "terrible twos" where they are touching everything, putting everything in their mouth, and--it seems--getting their source of life from pressing your buttons? And then the difference between ten-year-olds and the teen years--their adolescent years?

Puppies get that, too! Except, with puppies, you get hormone rushes at the same time as touching everything and the, "I'm not sure I want to listen to you," and the, "I know everything about the world!" bits. All of it. At the same time.

Welcome to the fun zone! Get your teeth-mark tattoo before you enter, and proceed to the left.

Puppies also go through fear stages, where the bigness and danger of the world come rushing back to them, and they're suddenly not sure about much of anything--including trash cans or inactive fire pits. (I speak from personal experience with that last example. And, as a point of interest, Cor had never seen the fire pit *active*. It was just a big metal thing that he was now inexplicably scared of.)

It is this roller coaster that you will be on for the first two to three years of your puppy's life. Be patient with yourself and your puppy--you are both growing, and learning.

Question: If you could tell someone going into this anything about what to expect from fear/adolescent stages, what would it be?

From FIGZ: *Poodle puppies go through several fear stages: at 5 weeks, 9 weeks, 5 months, and 9 months. Fear stages are sometimes obvious and sometimes it is barely a blip on your radar. It is important to keep things positive, without coddling, during all fear stages.*

5 weeks: The most impressionable of the fear stages. Be very mindful during this one. Anything that negatively implants during this stage can last a lifetime in a poodle. For example, if stepped on by a boot, the dog may fear or dislike boots for its entire life. If traumatized by a child, the dog may have aggression towards children or running and screaming for its entire life. We like to wait till puppies are out of this fear period before having lots of people, especially kids, visit.

9 weeks: This stage is a bit more subtle. This stage is usually coupled with the week they go to their new home. Many "new" things are happening this week: new home, new family, new sleeping area, new toys, new other pets, in addition to the first time away from the FIGZ family, their littermates, and other family and pets. We recommend limiting the amount of other "new" things during this time. If the puppy gets spooked by something during this time, you should not draw attention to it but rather divert the puppy's attention to something else. If the puppy reacts negatively to the "scary thing" DO NOT give a treat to the puppy as a diversion method. Treating will only set in the puppy's brain that the negative reaction was the positive thing to do. For most puppies, this fear period only lasts a couple of days, rarely the entire week.

5 months: We find this period rather comical but at the same very frustrating. The puppy may be hypervigilant towards objects or people that they have been around and fine with their entire life. Example: You are taking the puppy for a walk like you have done every day since having it, and when you walk past the bush at the end of the driveway, that has always been there, all of a sudden the puppy jumps 3 feet in the air. A simple, "leave it," and "let's go," and walking away as if nothing happened is your best remedy. This stage usually can get frustrating. It will seem like all your training, your dog's good healing, your confident dog, and all your hard work has gone up in flames. Just know this phase does not last forever but it will last longer than the other phases before now. This stage can last anywhere from 1 week to 2 months. This is the time when dogs will start to wash out of a program.

9 months: Hold on to your seat! As if the 5-month fear stage was not enough, here comes 9 months, and it is coupled with adolescence.

Girl poodles: Coming out of the 5-month stage and sometime around the start of the 9-month stage, your girl should hit her first heat cycle. (different genetic lines of dogs may vary). They can become emotional, irritable, tired, cranky, hungry, sassy, and fearful with all the new changes in their body, hormones, pain, and diapers. This is a hard time for training. Your girl may simply not want to do anything except lay around. It is also imperative to know that a girl's most prime time for getting pregnant is when her progesterone spikes. This usually happens between 10-16 days after the onset of her cycle. Boys will be able to smell her from down the block. This is a time you should not take her in public for training. If you must go out, be sure she is always wearing a diaper because during her cycle she also runs a high risk of contracting pyometra. Once the bleeding has stopped, she should be back to normal and the training session in public can resume. The phase lasts 21-30 days.

Boy poodles: This is a time when your sweet little boy will become the biggest jerk you ever met. Just like the girls, his hormones are coming in, and he may not be thinking straight anymore. He will become hypersensitive to smells. If he is a scenting service dog, you may experience a bit of a setback in him alerting you. He may start alerting for other people. He may become fearful of other dogs and humans—especially teenagers. He may even be challenged or attacked by other dogs, so parks and play dates should be limited. His natural instinct to take the "top dog" position in the pack will kick in. He may start to be *grumpy, pick on or even hump other family pets and children. This is also a time when he will naturally try to move from serving you as your service dog, into a guard dog for you.*

This is when having a trainer on-call is important. This is when you will need to be strong and confident for both you and your service dog. This is usually the time when most males fail their service dog training and are washed out of a program. How you handle him during this stage will either make or break his career as your service dog. Successfully navigating this period is like white water rafting. Hold on tight, use all your resources, keep your head up, and breathe.

From Amanda: A fear stage is a time in a dog's life when its brain chemicals are changing and maturing from the young puppy that they are and growing, and growing, and growing. Those fear stages come about to protect this young adolescent dog to understand that the world around them is not a fun and happy place--it is a scary place, where if they don't take note, they will die. That is a self-defense mechanism in the dog's brain to protect them as they grow and mature and not get killed by other things out there in the world, or get hurt. All of it is a self-defense mechanism. So, fear stages are very important in a dog's life, they're just really hard.

Now, a fear stage is sometimes pretty easy to spot. Your dog who was happy-go-lucky, working, and enjoying life, is now all of a sudden, scared of going out, nervous of a new scenario, freaking out over a new training tool--anything like that. Or, it's scared of the trash can that it walked by every day of its life. Many things can happen during the fear period that makes you think, "This is not my dog." That is the time in a dog's life to slow down. I say, take that time, go slow, pull back on training a little bit, let them mature, and let them get through this fear stage nicely, so that, after they're out of it, their brains are no longer telling them that everything in the world is going to kill them, and they're back to being the happy puppies they are. If you push through a fear stage to the point of exhaustion on their mentality, you're going to have a dog who is just never going to recover after they get scared of something, and that's not good for a service dog.

Now, the adolescence stage is different. Adolescence is just your dog's hormones coming into play. Whoo!

Puppies are innately driven to follow their people or their pack. When we have young puppies, a lot of people are like, "Our puppies are so great; they follow us everywhere, they're happy, they always come when called, and they just stay close to us--it's the best thing ever! We have the best puppies ever." And they expect it to stay the same for the rest of the dog's life. The adolescent stage is a time in that dog's life when their hormones are coming in, they are maturing and they are saying, "Hey, the world around us is cool and big; I'm going to go check it out," and they stop listening. They stop being that responsive puppy, they stop following you around, and they are now hormonal teenagers. And it's a pain in the butt because adolescent stages last for a good eighteen months. Minimum. Now, there are times in the dog's life when those hormone surges are more prominent and you're like, "Ugh, we are in a bad adolescent stage," but, honestly, an adolescent stage is from the six-month time frame to the two-and-a-half time frame.

Most are in the adolescent stage for two years. Dogs, mentally, don't mature until two and a half, three years of age for large breeds to giant breed dogs. Your small breeds mature faster because they don't go through as much growth so they mature a little faster, mentally. But, your large and giant breed dogs, take a while to mature, which is why labs are usually crazy until three, great Danes are usually stupid til three, and goldens are just crazy lovers for the rest of their lives.

The adolescent stage is a time frame in a dog's life where they just don't want to listen anymore, and it's not because they don't love you--a lot of people try to tell me that, "my dog doesn't love me!" It's not because they don't love you, and it's not because they don't respect you; it's because their hormones are telling them that they are big and bad, and they can find their fun, and they can think through their problems, and they are going to do whatever they want to do, now. They're no longer listening to you. So, the adolescent stages are a pain for most people because your dog is no longer the responsive puppy, and it's hard; you have to make sure that you are consistent, and you have to make sure that you set boundaries.

A lot of people don't realize that negative consequences are just as important in a dog's life as positive consequences, and it's just like kids and toddlers--you have to set boundaries.

8. Puppyhood

Question: If you could tell someone going into this anything about what to expect from puppyhood, what would it be?

From FIGZ: *Puppies are little balls of energy that also seem to sleep a lot. They can be excited, playful, happy, cranky, get zoomies, throw temper tantrums, and get overstimulated; very similar to a human toddler. When they get the zoomies, they just need to run. When overstimulated, they need a time-out. When happy and calm, they need a training session. It is very easy to get them to focus on you, usually with a treat added, and quickly learn commands.*

Puppies have short attention spans, so they need multiple small training sessions throughout the day to keep them engaged. Puppies need to sleep in between learning sessions so their brains can process what they have learned. Staying consistent with training and expectations will keep things clear to the puppy and help them overcome obstacles and fear stages. From a very early age, they will push boundaries. They will test your strength. Poodles, especially, are master manipulators and will try to overthrow the household. Be prepared for a bunch of cuteness, good markers being set easily, and yet a bunch of setbacks.

From Amanda: *People need to realize your puppies are with your breeders until the eight to ten-week time frame, which is great because they need to learn from their siblings. You don't want the dog to leave before eight weeks, because your dog is going to learn social cues and interactions with their littermates more than they will learn with you. That time with their littermates is going to teach them to bite inhibition and other things like that.*

The problem with puppies, though, is that they're puppies.

They don't go around the world touching things with their hands as toddlers do, they go around the world touching things with their mouths, because that is how they interact with things. The biting, nipping, and chewing, all of that is just how puppies explore. And it is the number one issue that everyone that gets a dog has, especially a puppy.

Working on bite inhibition is going to be one of those patience things. I always tell people that they need to have patience when it comes to nipping and chewing, and not to get frustrated. The more you get frustrated, the worse it's going to get, and the worse it's going to get for the rest of their lives.

Another thing that people need to expect with puppyhood is potty training; potty training is hard. For some puppies, it's very easy because their breeders set them up for success and they start potty training within that two-week time frame. It's great to start then and set them up for success for wanting a clean space; others, they don't get that start from breeders, so they do struggle with potty training. Don't expect potty training to be easy, because if you expect it to be easy, it's going to be hard, and if you expect it to be hard, it's going to be easy, and that's just how life usually works.

Another thing with puppyhood is the chewing factor. Puppies like to chew on anything and everything in sight; it falls into their mouth, and they're chewing on it. They're laying next to a wooden chair leg, and they're like, "Cool, this looks fun," and they'll chew on it. So, puppy-proofing is a big deal. Socks and other things like that puppies can swallow, and then, all of a sudden, you now have an obstruction, and you have to get them in for emergency surgery. You have to make sure you have it puppy proofed.

With puppyhood, you need to make sure you socialize the crap out of it. Refer back to my socialization timeframes. With puppyhood, you also need to make sure that you set them up for success with other animals and that they're not sitting there getting mauled by other dogs, they're not going to be mauled by the cats, they're not going to be picked on by other animals; you need to make sure you set them up for success, and you need to set boundaries with other animals.

Puppyhood is when your dog's mentality is at its very best. Honestly, your dog's brain is a sponge until sixteen weeks, and it's so easy to get caught up in teaching them basic obedience stuff, and not focus on everything else with puppyhood. And so, a lot of clients will have their basic obedience done quickly with their young dogs, which, again, is very easy to do, because their brains are sponges, and they learn like crazy, but they also forget to do all the other things, which is to make sure that the puppy is socializing, getting out there, and doing all the other things. So, I always say balance is the perfect way of raising a puppy; whatever you do basic obedience-wise as a timeframe--like, if you're spending ten minutes on basic obedience, you better go spend ten minutes on socialization that day, too, because the more you do outside of the house, the better they are.

9. Service Puppies are still Puppies

Up until now, I've been harping on the difficulties of owning a service dog, haven't I? That's not entirely fair. It doesn't mean the rest of the book is positive raving, but it's not all bad.

Yes, it's a living animal you get to take care of and have responsibility for, but they're also dogs, with all the wonderful goofiness that entails. So I want to take a bit of time here and tell a few stories to illustrate that, while these dogs are very much important medical equipment, they're also very much dogs. And, if you're owner-training or puppy-raising, puppies are still puppies.

Even a full-grown smart dog isn't standing, mentally, where a human does. They're learning and growing and--even when fully grown--trying to figure out how to fit their animal selves into our human world. We, humans, have a hard time integrating into other human cultures--imagine trying to cross special lines. From this, then, we get instances that certainly don't align with what most people inherently expect from service dogs, but that happens more often than most think, because, when not in the vest, service dogs are exactly that--dogs. Exceptionally well-trained dogs, but dogs all the same.

One of the big things that is important for service dogs to know is heel. In other words, walking nicely next to their human. This isn't easy for a dog--with all the smells and sights and sounds around, it's hard to stay in place and in step with their humans rather than running around sniffing and marking every post along the way.

Yaha had particular difficulty staying in heel rather than making sure the area was clear.

Well, there was a particular dog in the neighborhood he had problems with. We called him Armageddon. Every other consistent dog in the neighborhood he learned to be okay with, except this one dog (that looked very similar to him, I might add). When he saw this dog, it was like he had to warn the entire neighborhood the end was nigh and to get clear of the fallout. Of course, Armageddon had to say hello back. As our dogs said hi, Armageddon's person and I would exchange pleasantries as we both coaxed our dogs forward.

It was after one such exchange that this story takes place.

Armageddon and his person had turned the corner, and I could see our home a handful of houses down. Next thing I know, we're on the other side of the street, going the opposite way-- following Armageddon's vector of forward movement.

Remember those petite mal seizures? Yep. That's what gave Yaha the chance to notice I was no longer conscious of my surroundings and decide--on his own--that following Armageddon was far more interesting than going home. Acting on this decision in the span of the two to seven seconds I'm normally out of it, he turned into the road (maybe noticing no cars were coming), getting us both onto the sidewalk and going the other way before I came out of it.

Do you remember when I said service dogs had to know when to disobey their humans?

My trainer's response to hearing this story? That I needed to take someone with me on walks for a while, just in case something like this happened again, because it wasn't okay, and by the time I come out of it, it was too late to tell him that--he's already gotten away with it.

Go ahead, you can laugh. We do, often enough. These stories are funny, because, if they're not, you're going to find yourself mad and up in arms about far too much for your blood pressure as well as your dog's emotional state.

As I said, dogs are trying to fit into a completely different species' world. What comes from this is a tendency to not always understand what is wanted and when. I cannot tell you how many times this has happened. Most often, it shows itself when I have been training with Yaha or Cor, and they're doing whatever the task or obedience trait is, perfectly. I get out the camera to record them doing the thing and share it with my trainer to pass off on said skill, and when I ask them to do the thing they just give the camera this derpy look with their tongue lolling out and their head rolled to look over their shoulder. Even without vocalizing words, they are so clearly saying, "I have no idea what that means--I am just a dumb dog; I don't speak Hooman."

Things get even crazier when you throw them into a place or circumstance they're not used to. I have traveled back and forth between Texas and Wisconsin for a handful of reasons recently, and, as it turns out, just because dogs are house-trained for one house, doesn't mean they're house-trained for every house across the board.

Upon our first arrival, we pulled into my grandmother's driveway sometime around eleven-fifteen at night. I let him out to go potty, and we all went to bed. The next day we went and picked up food (dog and human), and made a few deliveries (I have a crochet business, and stuffing the final projects into the trunk was a lot cheaper than shipping expenses). That afternoon, we went and dropped some of my stuff off at my aunt's house, while she was at work.

Now, I want to preface this by saying that Cor has never had an accident in our house since one of his first weeks here, but within the first few hours at my aunt's house, he had had anywhere from three to five accidents. My aunt has had one or two other dogs have accidents in her house, which didn't help.

That's not all, though. In addition to the tinkling accidents at my aunt's house, he left a little present on my grandmother's bed *facepalm*. I have no idea how he got in there, because if I let him out of my sight that morning, it was for, at most, thirty seconds. But my grandmother walked into her room and did one of the little "oh!"s. You know, when you're surprised, but not quite shocked? She came out of her bedroom laughing. My mom and

I were kind of confused, because what could be in her room that is this surprising and funny? Turns out, a little present. You know how the emoji has a single pile with the perfect little spiral and it looks like you could pick it up without leaving a trace of the fact that it was there? Yeah. Right in the dead center of her bed. *dies under a rock*.

Speaking of my grandmother's house, when we first arrived, my grandpa was out fishing with some of his buddies; a trip he plans and looks forward to for just about the entire year. I was also going to be there for quite a few weeks. What this means, is that my grandpa didn't get there for a few days, so while we were there Cor could smell him, but didn't know where the smell was originating from.

Now, my grandparents have a large picture window looking right out into the Wisconsin woods. Cor had spent his entire life (at this point, eight months) in a Texas suburb where a 'forest' consists of three trees in a clump, and wildlife seen on a normal basis amounts to a couple of bunnies that have seen enough to know how to survive while passing their days taunting the dogs in the neighborhood. Compare this to the fact that my grandparents have had a black bear come to the feeders they have outside that window enough that, at this point, if it happens, they merely turn the lights off and watch. My grandpa shoots raccoons out the window. They admire the racks of bucks that come through and laugh at the birds and squirrels chasing each other away from the bird seed and deer corn (not for lack of trying to keep the squirrels away from the feeders, believe me).

As you can guess, for a dog whose ancestors were raised to hunt that ended up with an extremely low prey drive, watching the animals out this window was his favorite way to spend his time there (and, of course, he had to say hi). The only place that gave him the perfect view he wanted was a chair in front of the window--my grandpa's chair. Since I've been a kid, it's been understood that you can sit on the chair when Papa's not in the house, but when he comes in, he gets the chair, even if that means you have to move. End of discussion.

Well, that's all fine and good, but Cor didn't know that. So when Papa came home, Cor didn't understand why he had to give up the chair. Which led to Cor jumping onto it whenever Papa vacated it.

I say this with all the love in my heart, but this led to my grandpa and my service dog in training fighting over the chair like a couple of two-year-olds--as soon as one (Papa) left it, the other (Cor) claimed it. "Hands off, you have no more claim to it," kind of thing.

It was slightly amusing to watch, but not much help in assuring them that he was much more than a pet puppy.

I'm not saying they did, but I wouldn't be surprised if a lot of my family members in Wisconsin thought I was lying about him being a service dog simply due to what they saw inside the house.

That's the thing. When they're in the vest, they know they're working. When the vest comes off, it's like when my sisters and I would get home from school--most of the time, we were running low on our "good behavior" battery. And, when we got home, we didn't have to hold our behavior as tightly because home was a more forgiving place than school. Your dog knows that you will love them even when they act out and that they're not allowed to act out while in public because they're working. At home, there's a bit more leeway.

Speaking of fighting over something like a couple of two-year-olds, I've got another story for y'all.

Let me start by saying, I dogsit. So, most of the time, if it's an overnight thing, I'll bring Cor with me.

I got home from the visit to Wisconsin in the above stories on the thirtieth of October. We came to a rolling stop a few blocks from home, and I jumped out of my grandpa's truck and into my dad's Jeep and got to the voting polls minutes before early voting closed, to give you an idea of timing. Remember voting in the 2020 election?

On the second of November, I started dogsitting for Yaha for a week. Now, Cor thinks Yaha is the coolest thing since birth, and that "coolness" extends to his toys. So, while I brought Cor a couple of chews, what ended up happening is they would play "hot potato" with Yaha's antler. Just the one. There were, like, three, scattered around, not to mention Cor's chews, but neither of them were interested in any but this one antler.

Yaha would chew on it for a little, with Cor standing over him, watching. And then Yaha would get up for one reason or another, and Cor would snatch it and start chewing on it. A few minutes (or seconds) later, Yaha would wander over and stand over Cor, waiting for Cor to leave so he could chew it again.

Now, if this was just with Yaha, I'd think it was cute, right? Kind of like a sibling thing (he leaned into the tag-along little brother stereotype hard while we were there. I was laughing at those two so often because of the dynamic). But I almost think it's a jealous-little-sucker thing, because he did it again with another dog I was sitting for, and she dove into the game wholeheartedly, too. I sat for her on Thanksgiving as well as the week before Christmas, and they'd just keep tagging off with the antler almost consistently.

And that's another thing--Cor is a jealous little turd. He does well with other dogs--specifically female dogs, or those who don't look like him. He gets a bit overexcited with those who do look like him, and the way overexcitement comes out in him... well, it looks like something you'd think a male, unaltered dog would do with females. And yet, he hasn't tried it with any females or any dogs that aren't black like him since he was just starting to come into his own. And he knows a black female poodle who is just a few weeks younger than him, and he doesn't try anything with her. Because he's a little weirdo who can't hold his excitement *facepalm*. Welcome to adolescence, my friends. We're all on fire, here. Sometimes we mind. :)

Anyway, right. Jealous little turd. As I said, he does well with most dogs. I sit for several, and we've gotten together with a couple of friends from the program. He's fine. Lovely. Except... here's the thing. Okay, take that six-day dogsitting I did for Yaha. Cor can be curled up with the antler, happy as a clam. Yaha wanders over to me and asks for petting. Of course, I give it to him. It's what I'm being paid for, right? Besides, he will always have a place in my heart as my first service dog in training. And, let's be real. He's a dog not in a vest. I'm going to pet him.

At this point, though, Cor has noticed, so now he's coming over, trying to shove Yaha out of the way (there's, like, a thirty-pound difference between them, and it's not in Cor's favor, but you have to give him points for trying). He stands there, demanding attention from the same hand at the same time for the same amount of time.

In the same vein, at some of the outings, handlers will trade dogs, as it were, teaching them that they get to listen to the one with the leash. In case their handler can't be in control at one point and has to hand the dog off, or needs to focus somewhere else and have the dog obey whoever is there with them. Important things I never would've thought to practice-- another reason I can't suggest having a trainer's supervision on your way through this journey enough. Except, these dogs have been training with their handlers so much and consistently that, when this happens, unless they have either graduated or have religiously worked with others as well as their person, this throws all the dogs off. This is hilarious. You have all these dogs that are very exhaustively trained, and suddenly they're not obeying any command. At least for the first while; they start to get the hang of it after a bit. It gets even more interesting when you're working on recalls. You know, the "Cor, come!"

Let me paint the picture for you. We were working in Bass Pro Shop. We were in one of those aisles between the outdoor wall and the various end caps of different aisles. This was the day I was told he had too little confidence, so he'd be staying in Texas while I went to Wisconsin (which happened December 28, 2020).

I was working with a close-to-graduated dog, and could barely focus. In any event, he wasn't listening to me. Maybe he was able to tell I wasn't in a place to be the one directing this partnership. Besides, I wasn't his person.

After we did our recall, I ended up on the end of the aisle of dogs. The trainer working with Cor put him in a sit-wait and walked down the aisle to stand maybe ten feet from me before calling him.

He came, I'll give him that. Of course, as he was maybe another dog length from her, he sped up and tried to slither around her like the part-eel dog my sister is convinced he is. The trainer caught him, considering she's had four service dogs and is far from ignorant of the way dogs work. Like I said, though, he's a jealous little stinker. And smart. Way smart. Sometimes too smart for his own sake.

For instance, he knows better than to ask for pets when we're in public--all service dogs do--but that doesn't stop him, because he's cute, he knows he's cute, and he knows how to use it. We had brought Cor to one of our appointments, and he tried to get our doctor as well as our doctor's secretary to pet him. When we were in public at Natural Grocers near closing one evening, we were talking to the lady checking us out, and he turned around and looked at the lady at the empty register across the aisle, worked the cute, and wagged his tail. For as often as I have to tell people "he's working" (more than you'd think, unfortunately), I have to scold him for asking more than I should, as well. He knows better. And yet, there are times that, for some reason, he counts it worth trying. Not always--usually he's much better behaved than that, but still. Far too often.

Speaking of being too smart for his own good, (I've got several of these stories)... he has a favorite toy--it's a stuffed moose with a squeaker in the butt. Unfortunately, his teeth and jaws are getting stronger than they were as a puppy, so he is ripping the fabric much easier, at this point. So I have to take the time and sew up the nose or antler or whatever before I give it back to him. As I said, I run a crochet business, so I work with stuffing a lot and don't want him thinking that's okay to go after or eat, because I normally buy stuffing in bulk. In other words, I've got a lot of it. And I don't want him eating it because, even if that doesn't cause a blockage or cause him to throw up, that's kind of expensive dog poop. So, I don't let him play with toys that he has ripped to that point. I put it up on top of my bookshelf so I will remember I need to take care of it, but also so it is out of his reach.

...one would think. As I said, though, he's sometimes too smart for his own good. So, sometimes, when I think he's going and putting himself to bed--which he does, sometimes--he'll instead come trotting out with the moose in his mouth. And I do mean 'trotting'. You know the parade gait horses learn to do? Yeah, picture a poodle doing that, and you've got it. He'll come trotting out, and, once he knows I see him, he squeaks the butt. He did that with my sister Josie's stuffed otter for a while, too. He wouldn't rip or "play" with that one, really, just come trotting out and shake it in your face as if to say, "Chase the puppy."

In and out of the vest, service dogs are very much dogs and, deep down, puppies. They're goofy, they're silly, they're sassy, all the things pet dogs are. The smart and helpful aspects of their lives add added amusement, and, sometimes, frustration, when they are that goober of a weirdo.

Question: Do you have any stories of your dog that illustrate the differences between working and off-duty, or moments that make people wonder if your service dog is "actually a service dog"?

Out of vest, she bites anything that moves (that's the heeler in her) and talks back a lot at home. --Lauren Girsh
Clover LOVES people. When she's not working, she is the center of attention. She will beg you to pet her and give her belly rubs. She will also enjoy small puppy massages. --Sam

Despite Valor being a service dog, I tell people he is still a dog, especially when he isn't in vest and not working. When not working and if there's a squirrel in the backyard, you better forget about that recall for the next ten minutes because he will be busy barking at the roof. A rabbit went under the fence? He'll sniff that same spot for the whole day. As soon as his vest comes off, he rubs all along the couches as well. --Janet

At 9 months, JoJo typically gets a ton of compliments for being super polite and calm in public, but he still throws temper tantrums when he doesn't wanna come in from playing in the backyard. --Leonard Duncan

The fact that she is hyper and completely different here at home than she is when she's working and in her vest. -- Kelsey

Peach, when off duty, loves people. She will run up to them and lick them, and telling them she's a service dog makes them look at you like you're crazy, cause she's so in their face. --River

PETCO! Roo works exceptionally well in ANY store... except the Denton Petco. Which doesn't upset me, it's just really funny to watch her switch gears SO fast. --Kaleb Kelly

Question: How do your dogs de-stress after work?

Kennel and toy time. --Rose family
Cuddles and nap :) --Leonard Duncan
Nap. --Lauren Girsh
She wants to play, cuddle, or sleep. --Kelsey
Clover loves to chew on her Kong toy or her blue squeaky ball. Sometimes we play a kind of dog-version of soccer for about twenty minutes before we get ready for bed. --Sam
Fun time! Cuddles and love! --Anonymous
Lounging, zoomies outside, and cuddles with me. --Janet
We chase tennis balls and play tug of war. --River
Roo sleeps. We go for non-heeling walks at night. She also

gets some play breaks in the middle of the day during lunch when folks come over to my office to de-stress and play with Roo. --Kaleb Kelly

As soon as we get home from being out, Sugi goes straight out to the backyard and does zoomies. It's like he needs to get all that pent-up energy out from being in work mode. --Marleigh

10. Becoming Bombproof

Fully trained service dogs are what my trainer calls bombproof. That means that nothing should spook or faze them. This is what we're working toward through the socialization and desensitization periods of a dog's life, as well as during training. From ten to twenty-minute Home Depot or Lowe's runs at eight weeks, to the outings that our group has had at the Stockyards and mall, to the ability to behave themselves and work in an airport at the very end.

There have been outings in our program to the movie theater for the dogs to practice lying still and quiet--unless needed--during times when there are a lot of noises and lights. We have to get them around places they'll be expected to be--from church and baseball games to concerts and like I said, airports. A dog cannot be wary of a place to the point that they can't work; so, we have to get them out wherever they will need to be and make them, as I said, bombproof.

A large part of becoming bombproof happens during that first year and a half of their life with puppyhood, and how you handle fear and adolescent stages.

As I sit here writing and editing, Cor and I are smack dab in the middle of the adolescent stage and Cor has done much better at each of the outings we have been to most recently, and even I am starting to regain confidence that he is just in a stage where his ability and attitude change day to day rather than at risk of a wash. All that to say, we still haven't moved far enough along for me to assure you that he has pulled through his fear stages and is now a fully trained service dog--maybe in later editions. What I can tell you are some of the things that my trainers told me when I was starting to panic about him washing. Consider these next few pages something you can go back and reread when you're just... done. When you want to scream and cry and beg them to grow up. When you're terrified of what the bond you have will mean for your heart in the upcoming days and weeks and months. Because, while, yes, washing happens far more than anyone would wish, it's not always the result.

So, when you're having those moments of: "I've seen people with fully trained service dogs; surely this isn't one huge sadistic prank, right? I know people who have graduated. I have seen the posts come through that so-and-so and their dog has graduated. This is... this is a thing, right? I'm not in the Truman Show?" Let me assure you, it's not a joke. It's not a trick. This is a thing, and it has been for decades. Just because you haven't gotten there yet doesn't mean you won't. Gold and silver have to go through fire and heat to come out more than just pretty hunks of metal. I know it's cliche, but no pain, no gain.

Here we go: first, there's a huge difference between dogs at one year and two years. I must've heard this three to four times while we were standing there in Bass Pro Shop after hearing Amanda's verdict that we needed a break. According to my trainers (who have all seen numerous dogs through training), a dog doesn't get their "adult brain" until somewhere between twelve to eighteen months. As the adolescent that he is now, he's in the process of pushing boundaries and seeing what he can get away with. As I sit here, he's in the position of "dumb teenager" (it's a thing; I'm not that far removed from my teenage years, and I cringe to look back and see how moronic I was at times). He's full of hormones that he's trying to figure out the purpose of.

Second, they gave multiple examples of dogs who were hot messes at this point in their life who are absolute rock stars as they stand on the other side of "puppy brain." I would give you names, but they gave me so many that--beyond allowing the dogs and owners to retain privacy--I'm not sure I could recite them all.

Third, he turned one on January first. The outing took place on December twenty-eighth. For all intents and purposes, he was a year old; dogs are supposed to be in a fear stage around the one-year mark. The worst fear stage they have (and here I was, thinking he was through it).

The good news? This too will pass, and something new will come.

The news to work with? This too will pass, and something new will come.

But you know what? You'll make it through that, too. Because this is just part of life. This is part of the process--if it were easy, everyone would go through the training rather than just trying to fake a service dog.

You're still here.

Others have been here.

This is nothing new, and this is why you have a trainer--to get through things like this.

Foot Five:

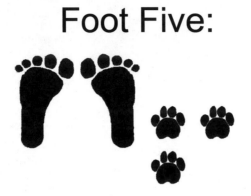

Rope Team

1. The Importance of Family

Okay. So. At this point, I think the size of the commitment you are signing on for, if you decide to go down this path, is starting to sink in, yes?

This next section is for handlers--just like the rest of the book--and families. But... mainly families. If you're having a hard time explaining what you need or asking for help, bookmark the start and end of this section, hand them the book, and tell them to read it. Or, better yet, hand them the entire book, and say you'll discuss it once everyone's on the same page.

Because this life is such a big commitment--especially if you're going the owner-training route--the importance of a rope team to keep you from falling too far if you slip on the path up the mountain cannot be overstated. Here's the thing. If you're owner training, not only are you trying to continue life as you have been up to now--something that is hard, as you're considering this route--but, in the middle of that, you're *also* taking on responsibility for a dependent. This is *hard*. THIS IS *HARD*. *THIS. IS. HARD.* I can't stress this enough. As an illustration, let's say you're climbing a rock wall blindfolded. Erik Weihenmayer climbed Everest blind in 2001, so this is possible. On a rock wall, you're climbing something that's meant to be climbed, which makes it easier. Similarly, people have trained service dogs before, but, even if you don't have a playing handicap, it's not easy. But you do have a playing handicap. Which makes the people holding your rope to keep you safe should you fall all the more important than they otherwise would be. Can you climb without a rope team? Technically, yes. But it's extremely difficult. That's what trying to train a service dog without a supportive family is like. It's possible, but you're going to be sweating the entire way, scared that sweat is going to cause your fingers to slip and make you fall. If you have a program, service dog doula, puppy raisers, or responsible breeders behind you, you may only fall to your last anchor, but you've still fallen, and gotten scraped knees and palms as a result.

If you're not just buying a fully-trained dog, you get to train the dog; you get to try and communicate a very acute need to a creature that doesn't speak English. If you are going complete owner training without the help of the saints that are puppy raisers, you also get to manage through fear, adolescent, and teething stages while working on training while continuing to fight your unique monster on a day-to-day basis. You will be going through something very similar to parenthood. It's not parenthood, but, according to parents in my life who are watching this process, it's very similar. This isn't just something to squeeze into your schedule a la extracurricular activities.

I have had times when I have told my dogs, "I love you; it's getting really hard to like you right now." I've had times where I've screamed "I want to like you!" in frustration. I've had days where things were going so badly, all I could do was look forward to bedtime. I've had days when one of my family members has told me, "I've got him; go for a walk. The long route. Take your phone and call Amanda. Go."

You will need time to just vent. You will need time to flee your lifeline--trust me, it'll happen. Service dog or not, medical equipment or not, you can't shove two living beings into the same space at the drop of the hat and tell them, "You live together now; go!" and expect there to be no problems at all.

You will get on each other's nerves. You will save each other. You will be all the other wants. There will be days where you can feel what they are feeling--physically, emotionally, mentally, whatever. It sounds weird, but it's happened to me multiple times. I think it has something to do with quantum entanglement...? I don't know; my sister can explain it far better than I can.

This is why having a supportive family cannot be underestimated.

In words directly from my trainer: *I am very much of the mindset that a service dog in a family setting, especially with young kids or teenagers, for instance--it's going to be a family effort to train this dog.*

We don't like working with anyone younger than twenty-one who doesn't have a supportive family, and that is because you're going to run into struggles. You're going to run into mindsets where you're not feeling like you're doing it well enough. You're going to hit depressive stages, and it is going to be up to the family members to step in and help out where you are failing; and, unfortunately, if you don't have a family who is willing to work, and train, and take it to outings, and do things with this animal, you're going to run into this aspect of "the dog will not work." It is not up to just one person to finish this dog, unfortunately.

Now, if we have an unsupportive family for anyone younger than, again, that twenty-one age mark--I say twenty-one because, yeah, you're legal at eighteen, but, honestly, you have a lot going on in your life when you first turn eighteen, so we still push until they're about twenty-one. But anyone who does not have a supportive family before twenty-one... we usually don't take them on as clients anymore, unfortunately. We ran into way too many problems where the kids--even the eighteen-year-old-- says they're going to do it, and they struggle. More often than not, they will struggle. Unfortunately, those dogs don't make it in the program because *of the unsupportive family members.*

So, just like sports scouts look at family members to see what they'd take on besides the athletes' skill, there are times that the families make or break the chance for the handler to get the help they need.

A family's role in this is no small feat: my family took on full responsibility for Cor for several months because all of us (specifically me, though,) figured I was the only one going through this--I was the only one shouldering the burden. And that had some negative repercussions we're working through, currently. The repercussions they dealt with, though, is a dog that, for nine months (almost ten), had not ever left my side, being without me for the foreseeable future. That includes preparing meals, grooming (standard poodle, remember?), training, and dealing with the everyday depression of something forever reliable being suddenly gone.

Even for those who aren't living in their parent's home, the importance of a family's support system is still a very real and important aspect. Again, from my trainer: *Now, if you are an adult with an unsupportive family member; again, if you're over twenty-one, paying your bills, doing your stuff, you know how to manage your own time by now, and you have these unsupportive family members, it is very unfortunate to live with.*

It is hard to work through all the scenarios, but, it's one of those things where, if you live on your own, it's not something that matters when it comes to the other family members. The hardest part is getting them to understand that the dog is needed for certain functions. For instance, my dogs don't go to certain family members' functions because I don't go to those functions, and I choose not to, because I need my dogs. And they understand that, but they also don't want them there, so it just is what it is, and I don't go. But, some people do choose to go to family functions without their dogs because there is only so much fight that we have. And so, when it comes to unsupportive family members, it is really hard and depressing to live with. You're not seen as an equal, anymore, I will say. You're not seen as someone that they want to be around, and it's not easy.

For some members of your family--for instance, my family, it took them a good few years before they realized I was disabled and understood that the dog wasn't there to just be something cute, it was there to work and help me. It's hard for families-- especially parents--to see their children change from these happy-go-lucky kids to these disabled adults, and that mindset is hard to come by, so, many parents struggle with that. It's not just that they're unsupportive, it's that they're having trouble. Again, my parents-- did not understand what Scout was there for. For a while.

I had him a couple of years and then he would come to town with me, but I wouldn't force us to take him places, because, again, I didn't want to go into why I had him. But my disability got so bad to the point where I needed him that I was no longer able to not take him, so, we had to have a really deep discussion and talk. My parents literally thought he was just a fake service dog, actually, for a while. Now they're very supportive, but... changing... I think change is the hardest thing with unsupportive family members.

For families in general, I just strongly urge people to not shun those with the dog. It is very easy to say, "Can we please leave the dog at home?" Because we as family, we as a service dog community especially, we understand going out in public with a dog means you're going to get more looks, you're going to get talked about, you're going to have people looking at you. For my family, that was hard. My mom hates--hates--being looked at in public; she has social anxiety, so it very much was a struggle for her for the longest time. And so, that was one of the reasons that I did not take my dog out in public with my parents as often, or I chose to stay home. An open conversation is needed to have an understanding in the family. I strongly urge family members to just be there as a support system, if they can. One of the things is that you want to encourage those with service dogs to keep going out to places, to keep doing the things they love to do, and to keep just being them. Because the dog doesn't change them, the dog just improves. It really does. And so, I always say, just be the support system they need. And if they need you to just vent with because their dogs are stupid, then just be there to vent with them. If they need you to drive them somewhere, drive them. If they just need love, then just be there for them.

Question: If you could tell the family of someone just starting on this road one thing, what would it be?

Allow them to vent, but also be supportive. This is a long journey and can be stressful and exhausting sometimes. --Kaleb Kelly

Stay with them. Help them. But also let them train their dog themselves. Help them where they need help but don't take over the dog. It is their dog who they need to train. --River

Be ready for the public; you can be rude! They will feel like a failure but they aren't, the dog will embarrass you A LOT. Have fun with training and just life in general with the dog. --Lauren Girsh

Patience! --Rose family

Be supportive, and if you have questions, then ask. A service dog is medical equipment, not a pet, and not an accessory. Asking someone to leave their dog at home for your benefit minimizes their condition and their need and gives the message that they don't need the dog, or their struggles aren't valid or important. --Marleigh

Support the handler. Even if you don't necessarily like the dog or even the idea of having a dog in your house, your handler is going through a huge change in their life. Please support them. --Sam

Please be supportive and encouraging. This is someone being brave and trying to take a big step in gaining their independence, and support from family would also help. My family would get angry with me because my training journey was taking longer than others and would compare me to others. Be kind, loving, and gentle; we are trying. --Janet

Be open to learning more, and accept mistakes as opportunities to learn. --Leonard Duncan

Just be very supportive; offer to help, and offer to be involved in any way that you can be without overstepping. Help them train, be an extra set of eyes to help them work on things that they're really struggling with. --Kelsey

Be supportive. Follow their instructions. Don't do anything outside of what the dog is allowed to do (jumping on people, taking food, etc.), and ask questions! --Anonymous

I think you can see the trend that I see. The support of the people around us means everything to us handlers. We know it's hard, but we see when you're trying, and even just trying to do something is appreciated.

We are not immune to the scoffs and judgement. Most of us will hear and feel them even when they're either not there, or not outwardly expressed. There will be people who judge us either because we don't look like we need a service dog, they don't see a service dog as more important than a pet, they think we can't see when they point and stare and whisper, or, they may just argue that we're being selfish.

None of this is nothing we haven't heard from our own minds, at one point or another. We've gone through the frustration that our medical equipment is still an animal. We've felt like sideshow attractions. We're no longer able to be invisible if we ever were. We hear the judgement. We see people waiting to jump on the first mistake our dog makes. We see the skepticism of those who only ever see the dog out of the vest, and wonder whether we're lying or just plain wrong. We see impatience. We see and hear it all, even if we don't mention it. Even if you think you're hiding it well--you're not. We see you. We hear you. We have become so accustomed to seeing the slightest shift in body language, in seeing the thought or preparation to do something in a dog's eyes, it easily transfers to being able to do the same to humans. People are not being subtle. The last thing we need is for our pit crew to be shoving nails in our tires.

If you have questions or doubts, talk to us.

Let us work through it.

Don't hide it and hope it'll go away--it won't.

How do you do this, though? Aside from what is offered--aside from the background, and more emotional help, what are practical things you could do to help the handler in your home? Or, if you're the handler reading this, what could you ask those around you to help with?

Glad you asked.

2. Families' Q&A

Contributing to this section of the book we have families of, and those who have lived with...
River and Peach
Scooby-Doo and his handler
Luna and her handler

Question: On a scale of one to five, how supportive do you consider your family? If you answered the previous question anything other than one, in what ways do you support the handler?

Note: out of courtesy and privacy, I will not be labeling who put which answer. If names are offered in the answer, however, I am leaving them in.
Five: 100%
Two: I help with videos and transportation to public lessons
One: I do almost everything myself, except when I'm home [from college]. My mom will take Luna out in the mornings if I'm not awake because she's already up and it's easier than waking me up. Other than that, I do everything else, all the training, grooming, pottying, feeding. My parents have been very supportive of me, though, and when I couldn't drive, my mom would drive me to Dallas to do outings with Scout's Legacy. They have also helped me pay for Luna's training. My grandparents are also very supportive, even if they don't quite understand why she's so useful to me.

Question: What was something you expected in this journey that didn't happen?

I expected to encounter more badly trained dogs (that's not to say that we haven't encountered them). Part of that might be because I go out of my way to avoid other dogs in public. --Luna

I expected my daughter to keep the dog with her 100% of the time. --Scooby Doo

He can't find a job as no one wants to hire a minor with a service dog. --Peach

[Note: I direct you back to the illegality of denying someone a job just because of a service dog.]

Question: What was something you didn't expect to happen in this journey that you are glad you did?

I have watched my handler become a great dog trainer. --Scooby Doo

I'm glad I got to meet so many cool people through Scouts Legacy; I came for a service dog and ended up with a family. --Luna

All of the friends and support we've received from our service dog company. --Peach

Question: What was something you didn't expect in this journey that you wish hadn't happened?

Trying to film videos every week is very stressful. Especially the ones that require a stranger to participate. --Scooby Doo

I wish that people wouldn't harass me when I'm out and about with my dog. --Luna

Question: What do you hope your handler's dog never loses?

His sweet personality. --Scooby Doo

Her excitement to work and her love to do things for me. --Luna

Her life or ability to work, as it would crush my son. --Peach

Question: What do you hope your handler's dog grows out of?

Crying whenever the handler leaves the room without him. Barking for attention if he feels ignored. --Scooby Doo
Stealing and eating towels. --Luna

Question: If you could tell someone going into this life anything, what would it be?

This will not be an easy journey or a short one. There are no shortcuts to the finish line. --Scooby Doo
Do a ton of research, and see if you can shadow someone who already has a service dog for a day just to see what it's like being out in public with a service dog. Dogs aren't robots, and you shouldn't expect them to be; mistakes are bound to happen, the crucial thing is to make sure you turn the mistakes into a learning experience. --Luna
The training never stops, even when you purchase a "fully trained" service dog. --Peach

Question: If you could tell the family of a future handler anything, what would it be?

The relationship between the handler and the service dog is unlike any other relationship. The bond goes way deeper than the pet/owner relationship. --Scooby Doo
Remember that the dog is still a dog and is allowed to be and remind its handler to step back and never deal with the dog when mad or frustrated, as it only makes things worse. --Peach

Question: Is there anything you would like to add that I didn't ask about?

What dogs can do is amazing. Peach has added so much to all of our lives and we are so grateful for her. And remember that not all service dogs are purebred. Peach is a mutt. --Peach

3. A Letter to the Supportive Family

I want to talk to those of you who are living with someone getting a service dog, now. Those of you who believe your family member does, indeed, need a service dog.

You're not getting the dog, right?

It's going to be their medical equipment, right?

It's their responsibility, right? After all, isn't that what I've been saying?

Well, yes, but actually no.

I want you to think about everything you do in your day-to-day life that affects those around you. Here's a bit of a list to get you started:

--Have a job/go to school.

--Are married/have kids/are a kid/live with someone.

--Have an extracurricular activity/do something after your job/work.

--Eat

--Sleep

--Watch TV/play video games

--Have a hobby

Okay, I'm going a bit far on this, right?

Mmmm... think again. All the abovementioned things you do is what a dog is going to do that will affect you.

Let me break it down for you.

--Have a job/go to school.

If you're an adult with kids and you have to get to work before they can go to school, you have to come up with a way for them to get to school, right?

Maybe you're an adult with kids and you can arrive at work after dropping your kids off at school. As long as they get to school at a certain time, right? Which means you have to leave at a certain time. Which means they have to get up and get ready at a certain time.

Okay, well, what if you're not the adult in this equation--maybe you're the coolest thing on the planet: someone who can drive themselves where they need to go. You don't have to depend on anyone else, right? You're in-de-pen-dent.

Wrong. You driving yourself means there's one less car at the house.

You're going to school or work means your presence or absence makes a difference both at home and at the building you're going to. If you're to school on time, you aren't interrupting the class by walking in late. If you're late, you're affecting people's day. If you are at work, other people have to do less. If you're not, they have to do more.

If you work or go to school, it affects your family's financial standing.

If you work or go to school, it affects others.

A service dog will have to work and go to training. It will affect you just like you will affect it and its handler.

A service dog (and, likely, their handler,) will need rides to the training and outings that the dog needs to keep active and mentally in the right place to help their handler.

--Are married/have kids/live with someone.

I feel like this one goes without saying, but let me break it down into more acute details you may not have thought of.

Do you affect people when you get sick? So will the dog.

When you go to sleep or wake up affects what others can and can't do--you can't practice your heavy-metal band's song while someone is sleeping, can you? Maybe acoustic guitar, but heavy metal... yeah, that'll get your neighbors calling the cops on you. When a puppy is sleeping, it's kind of like a baby sleeping--don't wake the baby! ...dog. The baby dog.

The amount of room necessary varies when there are more people in the house. Same with a dog.

Your mood impacts the people you live with--whether you have anger issues, are in a weird mood where everything you say is a joke, or are in an "I'm tired of your faces" mood or an "I need people around me" mood--your mood impacts those around you. Why shouldn't another living creature?

--Have an extracurricular activity/do something after your job/work.

Whether it's soccer, band, reading, writing, cooking, or sitting and watching TV to blow off steam, whatever you do after school or work affects those around you. Whether it's being in a hurry to get to a game/performance on time, leaving you alone, or--in the case of cooking--getting something they enjoy out of it; there is nothing you do that doesn't affect other people. Especially if you're in the same house.

--Eat.

I'm going to explain this in the form of a math problem. You have a whole pie. You're the only one who needs some. How much do you get? The whole lovin' thing.

Someone else has the pie and you want some. They decide they're okay with sharing. How much do you get? Half.

Now, what if that other person had a party of ten, including you, that they were sharing with? How much would you get? A tenth.

Your eating affects others.

So, yes. The puppy is going to impact you, but everyone impacts others throughout their day.

And--little secret, here--this dog will subtract from the effects the human handler has on your life. I--and the service dog owner living in your home--no longer need service humans because we have the service dog. My family no longer has to be on high alert for my seizures and joint malfunctions, because Cor will tell them when I'm having a seizure, and can help me when I need it. Same with the situation in your house.

Yes, the dog is mostly the handler's responsibility-- they'll be the ones picking up puke and accidents, training and disciplining. Yet, it being their responsibility doesn't mean no one else gets to help. I need dogsitters every once in a while, and so will the handler in your house. Whether it's so they can go somewhere the dog isn't ready for, or just because the dog and handler need a break from each other, there will be times others in the family need to step in. And, let's be honest, a dog is coming into the house--there are benefits for everyone from that, right? :)

Question: If there was anything you could tell a family (or other support people) who are supportive of someone going into the service dog life, what would it be?

From Amanda: *For my supportive family members, I urge them to understand that they need to learn how to work this animal as much as the handler themselves, because heaven forbid anything happen, and you have to step in and work the dog because the handler is not able to, or they had to walk away for a second. This dog needs to be able to work with everyone, so the more family helps and participates, the better this dog gets.*

4. A Letter to the Unsupportive Family

For the family that doesn't think the handler needs a service dog, I have a question. What could they have to gain from pretending they need this dog?

Attention?

Trust me when I tell you that the attention that naturally comes from having a service dog isn't the kind people want. Not when it's a fully trained service dog. It's so much easier to just buy the vest and pretend--which is a whole other rant, believe me. (That's coming later.)

I understand you may not entirely understand the reasoning behind their choice, but trust me when I say it's not a decision made lightly. For that, I give you the reasons that I will give and have given them for why they need to think about whether they want it.

Money.

Time.

Unwanted attention and scrutiny.

Being misunderstood.

I want to take a second and pause on that last one because I don't say it flippantly. I don't mean misunderstood in the way many apply to storybook "villains" or so many others (which is a whole other rant I'm not going to get into here). What I mean is something any service dog handler knows about--people assuming they know why you need the dog or that the dog means you want to talk.

This is especially troubling for my friends with PSDs-- psychiatric service dogs. These are the dogs that are actively trained for anxiety or depression along with the better known Veteran PTSD dogs. These are dogs for things that, like my seizures and other autoimmune paraphernalia, are not visible. And that's what trips people up. What, I would imagine, is tripping you up. The invisibility of the monsters they're fighting. Not only are they going through what you do on a normal basis--no small feat, I am sure--but they are actively fighting their bodies to be able to do what you take for granted--get out of bed, on some occasions. Order from a restaurant.

And that's where the "for attention" comes into play, isn't it?

Let me ask you something. Why, if they wanted attention, would they go about trying to get it like this? If they're lying about needing a service dog to help fight a nonexistent monster, that becomes an extremely costly lie.

Here's another way of looking at it.

When you bring a dog into public, you are signing a nonverbal contract, as it were--I will remain in control of this dog. It can handle itself in public. And the vest is so iconic, so eye-catching, that it comes with even heavier expectations. That is extremely stressful. It is exhausting for me, and I don't have social anxiety. For my friends who have trouble getting themselves to go out in public, adding a living being to be responsible for on top of that--and the fact that you are now most noticeably not invisible, especially if your monster is--that simple outing to get milk becomes a verifiable battle.

Instead of this series of actions:
--notice you're out of milk
--sigh annoyedly
--check that it fits your budget to spend what milk costs
--find your wallet
--grab your wallet
--find your keys
--grab your keys
--get in the car
--start the car

--drive to the store
--go in
--grab the milk
--check out
--come back out
--drive home
--use the milk to make the cookies you wanted

You have this series of actions:
--notice you're out of milk
--sigh annoyedly
--find your wallet
--grab your wallet
--find your keys
--grab your keys
--grab the treats
--grab the vest
--grab the leash
--call your dog
--put the leash on the dog
--get the dog in the car
--take the leash off the dog
--get in the car
--start the car
--drive to the store
--get your dog out of the car
--put the vest and leash on the dog
--go in
--answer/ignore ten comments people make about "doggy,"
"oh, he's so cute!", "my dog isn't that well-behaved at all."
--grab the milk
--answer/ignore twenty more comments
--check out
--come back out
--take the vest and leash off the dog

--get the dog in the car
--drive home
--bring the dog inside
--use the milk to make the cookies you wanted--if you still have the energy to do so

Even a simple outing becomes much harder. When you don't answer the questions, you have to try to pretend you don't notice the stares.

If you are willing to answer questions (like I am a lot of the time, simply because I can), you answer a lot. Multiple times, many of them. Either way, you end up dealing with a lot of people that, while they wouldn't just walk up to a dog being walked down the street, seem just fine walking up and petting a service dog without asking. I refer you to the air tank/walker scenario mentioned earlier in the book. (Ask the person who handed you the book to point it out.)

If you're lying about a medical situation for attention, lie about a broken leg--not needing medical equipment that costs hundreds of dollars a month.

If your family member says they need a service dog, nothing you bring up will they not have thought of. You aren't clever--you aren't catching them in a lie. This is an invisible battle they're fighting, and the least you could do is not boo and throw tomatoes from the sidelines.

On behalf of all my friends in need of PSDs... knock it off. Thank you.

Foot Six:

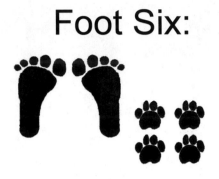

Price

1. Count the Costs

So. You do need a service dog for a verifiable medical reason, be it mental or physical.

One of the things you have to decide in training a service dog is how you want the dog trained--owner-training? Fully trained? Puppy raiser? Do you want to do it some other way?

To figure out which version will best fit your needs and desires, you have to ask (and answer) a few hard questions. HONESTLY.

Aside from those already brought up, are you able, ready, and eligible to learn how to train your dog from a trainer's tutelage?

Are you able to hold to the fine print on any or all of these methods?

How much time can you honestly devote to training, playing, petting, etc.? You are basically bringing home a baby that will remain dependent for several years. You are bringing home a flesh and blood creature that will affect every area of your life.

Are you ready for every single area of your life to change? You will never again be completely alone. Yes, the puppy will nap, but you get to adjust your life around that, because when they're awake, you get to keep your attention on them--they will get into trouble, and they will need you to help them because puppies don't just inherently know that this or that is bad for them.

If you work outside of the house, you will have to figure out how to incorporate them--do you leave them at home and hire a dog walker and then devote time when you get back home to training, playing, and releasing their energy--daily? Do you bring them with you and somehow keep them behaved?

If you work at home, is your job flexible enough that you

can work around their nap schedule?

If you have kids that have after-school activities, how does the dog factor in? A dog sitter? Can you bring them?

Are you able and willing to commit to this financially? Again, if you're getting a puppy from a breeder, prices get up into the thousands--you're paying for the ancestors, the postnatal training, the food, socialization, sleepless nights, and postnatal vaccines, not just the living creature. If you're buying from a rescue, you may be saving money, but you're paying with the uncertainty regarding the aforementioned aspects people pay breeders for.

Training is at least as much--my trainer's charges are on the low end of the spectrum, and owner training is on the low end of that spectrum (in that you're paying it over several months and not all at once), and I am still paying $5,000 total, which I am paying in $200 monthly payments.

And then there are the various toys, treats, chews, food, leashes, collars, grooming sessions (or tools, if you're like me and are willing to learn how to do the thing to save a bit of money), and other supplies that you need. Not to mention vet bills. This is no small monetary commitment, and if you choose to go this path, it doesn't stop. It's a big commitment money-wise, that you get to figure out how to make every time--whether that's a monthly payment or every time you want to buy the adorable little rascal a chew toy so he doesn't keep thinking your shoes or sleeves are the best options to soothe his aching gums, jaw, and teeth. This can easily amount to another $200 per month--largely due to training treats.

Each of these numbers varies depending on the dog and handler. For example, Cor is rather picky about food--he prefers a raw food diet to kibble. I have found a way to order his raw food in bulk, so it's less expensive, but every few days I have to cut the five-pound tubes into pucks to give him throughout the week/ month/fortnight, depending on how much I cut up. With Yaha, I'd spend nearly $100 on antlers alone each month. My budget took a digger, but it saved our shoes, furniture, and remotes; thus, it saved our deposit on our rental.

A safe number to estimate would be anywhere from $400-$500 per month (that's keeping training at about $200 per month). That number will be impacting your budget every month until you pay off training--when it will decrease. It will never not be a part of your monthly expenses, though. Think about that-- truly think about it.

Are you willing to accept that condition of having a service dog? I was. I didn't know how I would pay every month, but that was something I was willing to figure out as I went. What about you?

At what point is this commitment no longer worth it? Find it. Build a wall on top of that line. This can't be a line drawn in pencil that a cute, ears-too-big-for-its-face puppy can push over. If this doesn't fit in your life, it doesn't fit. Don't do you and the dog more damage by trying to push through. It will cause damage-- more than it would to try to figure something else out. If it doesn't fit, either acknowledge that and move on, or rearrange some things in your life to make it fit. You're putting rocks and sand and water in a jar. This is a rock--not sand. It won't move around to accommodate you after you've put the other two in.

Question: If you could tell someone going into this anything about finances, what would it be?

From FIGZ: *Service dogs are expensive! If you train or buy a fully trained service dog, be prepared to spend approximately $35,000 - $45,000 on the service dog for things including, but not limited to housing, food, treats, toys, clothing, gear, leashes, vests, collars, training classes, private instructors, medical supplies, bills, health insurance, transportation, and more. Keep in mind, because service dogs are medical devices, they may be payable by insurance and can be taken on Schedule A income tax forms as a medical deduction for the entire life in which the service dog performs its duties.*

From Amanda: *For the finances of a service dog, you have to look at the whole picture. If you are owner training, for instance, you have to look at the cost of the dog, which is up to three thousand dollars, if not more. Then you have to look at the cost of training; every trainer and training program is very different. Training could be anywhere between the five thousand to fifteen thousand dollar range for owner training, depending on who you're working with. Then you have to look at the everyday life of living with a dog, and that is your food costs--because dogs need to eat--vet bills, treats, chews, your daily supplies, your dog gear. People think that owner training is cheaper because they're not dropping the twenty grand, but in reality, you're just paying that twenty-five thousand payment over the two years that you have the dog.*

Other things to consider for finances would be the emergency costs of a dog, because dogs are going to have a good and bad day, and puppies are going to make mistakes. So you're going to end up seeing the emergency vet once in a dog's lifetime. And that can range anywhere from fifteen hundred dollars to five thousand dollars range depending on the emergency. If your dog has bloat, for instance, you're looking at twenty-five hundred dollars. If your dog has an abscess in its stomach. Anything that can happen probably will because that's how life works. So emergency vet funds are a thing that people should consider when they are looking at adding a service dog to their home.

2. Time

A lot of what I have constituted as "cost" so far has been tied to money. But that's not the only cost you need to come to terms with.

Just like anything you commit to, there are emotional, mental, physical, and timing costs, as well as financial ones.

To illustrate, let's say you're making cookies to celebrate... I don't know, I'm writing this on the twenty-first of December, so let's say you're making Christmas cookies. As you're making them, you realize you finished the last of your milk with your cereal and the candy cane you had for breakfast. (Hey, we've all had those days. You'll have them if you have a dog, too.)

So now you have to go get milk.

Without a dog, the steps you'll have to take to do so may look something like this:

--notice you're out of milk
--sigh annoyedly
--find your wallet
--grab your wallet
--find your keys
--grab your keys
--get in the car
--start the car
--drive to the store
--put in earbuds so you don't have to talk to anyone and can get back home before the oven is done preheating (optional, I suppose)
--go in
--grab the milk
--pay for the milk

--come back out
--drive home
--use the milk to make the cookies you wanted

With a service dog:
--notice you're out of milk
--sigh annoyedly
--find your wallet
--grab your wallet
--find your keys
--grab your keys
--grab the treats
--grab the vest
--grab the leash
--call your dog
--put the leash on the dog
--get the dog in the car
--take the leash off the dog
--get in the car
--start the car
--drive to the store
--put in earbuds so you don't have to talk to anyone and can get back home before the oven is done preheating (hey if you did it before...)
--get your dog out of the car
--give them the opportunity to go potty so they don't have an accident in the store --put the vest and leash on the dog
--replace the earbuds that fell out
--go in
--answer/ignore ten comments people make about "doggy," "oh, he's so cute!", "my dog isn't that well-behaved at all." (Because people are more able to see the dog than the earbuds.)
--grab the milk
--pay for the milk

--answer/ignore twenty more comments

--come back out

--take the vest and leash off the dog

--get the dog in the car

--drive home

--bring the dog inside

--use the milk to make the cookies you wanted--if you still have the energy to do so.

Reading that, it may not look like there's a lot more you have to do with a dog than without one, but, at the moment--especially on one of those days (may I remind you of your supposed breakfast of cereal and a candy cane?) it can get overwhelming very quickly. Yes, the dog can help with that, but I would also warn you not to underestimate the stress that taking a not-completely-trained dog into public can give you.

Mentally, you're going to be doing a couple of things in that moment of being out.

Number one, you're in public getting milk.

Two, you're keeping an eye on your dog to make sure they're behaving.

Three, you're either answering--or trying to ignore--questions or comments from passersby who assume you're ready and willing to talk because you have a dog with you.

That's when the dog is trained to be able to go out with you; that won't always be the time cost people in the home get to pay. There are also time costs in the realm of:

Who keeps track of vet records?

Who takes the puppy to the vet?

Who cleans up accidents out of both ends--they will happen. If it's in the middle of the night, does the person responsible change?

Who trains the dog?

Who picks up dog poop?

Who takes the dog for walks?

Who plays with the dog when people have homework and work?

When people have extracurriculars?

Who keeps up with the trainer?

Who keeps tabs on the puppy's bowls and makes sure they've eaten and had enough water?

Who makes sure the puppy has pooped? (A lot of times, this is the first sign something is wrong.)

Who takes the snotty tissues and used hygiene products out of puppy's mouth when they get and parade around with them, demanding attention (this WILL happen--they smell like you they *must* be delicacies, right)?

Who does all of this when the handler can't?

Take it from me, raising a puppy is no easy feat, and neither is juggling all the daily requirements that you also have to fit into your day. These are all questions you may not be able to answer when they need to be answered--these are questions you need to think of before they happen. If the puppy throws up in the middle of the night for no reason, (it happens. Happened once every few days for a handful of weeks, to us. Of course, then I realized the problem was a specific toy I was letting him play with...) and your stomach can't handle the smell or sight of it, and you can't do it, what happens? Do you wake someone up? Do you wait until morning and let the smell soak into the floor? Do you suck it up, buttercup, and hope you can get to the bathroom in time to nip in the bud the need to clean up two piles?

What if you come home from work or school and the puppy is too young to go with you, and is now going crazy and needs to go for a walk or romp in the backyard but you have so much work or studying that you're not sure you'll finish even if you start *right now*?

What if you're in the middle of a class on your computer at home and your puppy decides that it's awake now, and needs to play? When you can't, because of your studying or work, what happens when the puppy decides it'll entertain itself and starts pulling everything that's not nailed down off the shelves? You may have trained them not to, but you're ignoring them, and they need attention now.

What if they swallow a sock or underwear (again, it smells like you, therefore it is the most interesting thing in the world) and you have to take them to a vet, but you have a prior engagement? Who drives them to the vet and stays with them? Who pays for the vet bills if your emergency fund isn't big enough?

3. Fake Service Dogs

There are other costs, too. Most of them you can't control. Think of it like this. You're on the thirteen-year walk of an adventure, and one of the towns you have to pass through has a protest or riot blocking the only road out of town. You can't fix the riot, so how do you handle it?

As I said before, there is no registry for service dogs--you do not need to get "certified" or "register" a service dog. If it is told to you that you do, or implied in any way, that person is lying to you and what you are looking at is a scam.

Because you don't need to register for a service dog, and there is no federal test you have to pass or anything of the sort, it becomes very easy to fake a service dog. The vests aren't expensive, and neither are the patches. There are even people who make custom patches for service dogs, and it's not like they can ask for proof of completion of the course. For less than fifty bucks, you could make your dog look like a service dog, and, coincidentally, get them in just about anywhere, because very few people know they can question a service dog, and even fewer are willing to.

No, I'm not kidding; a service dog can be questioned. Legally.

Managers of stores or other public places are allowed to ask two questions to confirm a dog in a service dog vest is either a service dog in training or a fully trained service dog. "Is this a service dog to help with a medical disability?" And, if they're still unconvinced, "What services does this dog perform?"

Please note that "he makes me feel better" is not an adequate answer. Permissible answers are to the tune of "he picks stuff up for me when I can't get it," "she hears for me," "he grounds me during anxiety/PTSD attacks," "she alerts me to oncoming seizures," "he is a diabetes alert dog," "she pulls my wheelchair," "he does counterbalance," and several others. Long story short, a handler of a real service dog will be able to answer this question.

If they aren't able to answer right away that does not mean they cannot answer. It's unnerving, being put on the spot like that, and some people go nonverbal when having anxiety attacks. If they truly cannot give a suitable answer, though, or the dog gets out of control, businesses are allowed to tell handlers to leave. This does not constitute a ban--it simply means that, until the dog can be controlled, or you can give a satisfactory answer to the above questions, you have to leave; just like if businesses ask people without furry sidekicks to leave. Also important--a dog throwing a fit or giving a single bark does not constitute an "out of control" dog.

Oh, and, if and when people lie about their dog being a real service dog, everyone can tell from the dog's behavior. I refer you back to the two-year training and the price. And, yes, stores are allowed to kick these people out, too. In fact, everyone except those trying to cheat their dogs into stores is grateful when they do this--including the real service dog handlers. We would gladly answer these questions if it meant a decrease in fake service dogs!

These fake service dogs give real service dogs a bad name, and the ignorance most people have when it comes to their rights in dealing with these fake service dogs, or out-of-control dogs, lead to a supposed need for service dog legislation. This is not needed, and could very well harm the wide array of people who benefit from service dogs.

There are times when a vest or leash hinders a service dog from being able to do its work. This is why the ADA states that, if it doesn't interfere with the dog's tasking, the dog must wear both when in public (read: places that are not normally dog-friendly). If it does interfere with their work, however, they are not required.

This is why service dogs being trained to walk in heel, their ability to heel off leash, and why their behaving and being able to work while not in vest is so imperative. Because, if someone needs them to stay in one spot while their handler is out of sight, they have to be able to. If their handler needs them to get help, their handler can't be holding the leash the entire time.

Fake service dogs not only cast doubt on the behavior and skill of other dogs people see in public, but they can also do far more damage, both to the dog, the handler, and, quite possibly, their person. There are numerous stories of service dogs being mauled or killed by dogs people took out in public that are dog- or human-aggressive. Under the ADA it is illegal for a human or dog to harm, kill, or harass a service dog or their handler. This is punishable by a fine and jail time. As I stated before, you wouldn't pull someone's walker out from under them, or pull someone's oxygen tubes out of their nose. Service dogs are medical equipment, too.

Again, some people are allowed to question a service dog handler. A regular passerby may not, but if you see a dog you suspect of being a fake service dog, *please*, talk to a manager and ask them to address it. Again, we would all be willing to answer these questions if it protects against fake service dogs.

Now. I'm going to take a bit of a rabbit trail, here. It is permissible to ask an out-of-control dog to leave. It is permissible to ask a handler who can't answer the two questions to leave. It is not legal under the ADA to tell someone they can't come into a place because they have a service dog, save for the places of worship and must-be-kept-immaculate areas mentioned previously. This, unfortunately, doesn't mean it's not done.

In the state of Texas, if someone charges you with criminal trespassing, that takes precedence over the ADA's "can't be denied entrance". My training group found that out after they had a run-in with a store that threatened to do just that. The cops showed up and everything. Now, the trainers and police talked and everyone parted ways with no tickets given and a lesson learned. However, my point is to research the allowances/ precedents in this area in your state/country/province so you don't get in trouble. Not everything--very little, in fact--is cut-and-dry when it comes to service dogs. You can't do enough research.

Question: As someone very deep in the dog world on the whole, can you share your thoughts on fake service dogs?

From Amanda: *The hardest thing is that fake service dogs are affecting the entire world; it's not just the US, but the US does take the biggest brunt of it, because of how lax our laws are. The biggest problem I have with fake service dogs is going to be the ones that are out there, aggressive, and having problems, but, unfortunately, aren't being dealt with according to the law. Because there are laws in place to kick those dogs out, and there are laws in place to reprimand the handler, but people aren't using those laws, and going after the people who are being the problem. So, in my perfect, ideal situation, we would just follow the laws we have, and better educate the workplaces, so that way they can follow them.*

Now, to me, anyone who is taking a dog out in public, letting it run amok, and having it not behave; I mean, that's a fake service dog. Whether or not you have a disability, that doesn't mean the dog is immediately a service dog. The rule of thumb is disability plus task-trained dog equals service dog. If you don't have a disability, but you have a well-trained dog, that's not a service dog. If you have a disability and have an untrained dog, that is still not a service dog. There is a fine line between what is and what isn't expected of our animals, and the service dog definition.

4. Love is Blind; You Cannot Be

I'm sure we've all heard the saying, "Love is blind." That can very easily be the truth when you have your dog whose ears are too big for their body and who thinks they're tough enough to take on the vacuum or rake. Or even poop bags. The thing of it is, though, when you're trying to train this ball of fluff to be a service dog, being blinded by love is a very dangerous thing. Something that will quickly display where your pup needs to improve is simply asking someone who is living with you what they see that could be improved. Be warned--if you do this, you have to be ready to get answers you're not necessarily going to like.

Other times, life just tells you what the team's shortcomings are.

When I took Cor up to Wisconsin, his problem with getting so excited that he would jump up on people became even more clear than it already was, because my cousin... well, she's not exactly a heavyweight contender. The fact that he has a thing for "victory laps" and disregarding boundaries also became clear, as neither of the places I was staying had a fenced-in yard. So it became a matter of course that when he had to go out, I had to put a leash on him. When he was playing outside he had to be on a long leash, something he did not like. Again, going back to the preferred to not listen to boundaries.

When I thought Cor had made it through a fear stage, I took him out for a group outing and he had his tail low and was slow to respond to commands the entire time--apparently, we weren't out of the fear stage as much as I'd thought.

If you are going to take a dog out into public, they have to be able to handle themselves. You can't be letting them get away with murder. The best person to ask how your dog is doing is your trainer. Again, they've been through this before, and they are not nearly as emotionally entangled in your dog succeeding as you are. Don't get me wrong, they don't want either of you to fail, but, chances are, they're not as likely to break down as you are if your dog doesn't make it. Therefore, they can look objectively at the situation as a whole. Ask your trainer. They aren't pulling for you to fail. They aren't trying to put you or the dog in a bad place. Their success as a company and organization is directly proportional to how good they are at helping you and your dog succeed in this area. They want to help you. Ask your trainer.

Question: What are the most common things you have noticed people don't see in their own dogs?

From FIGZ: *Allow your dog to be a dog! They need a break, a day off, time away from the job; just like we would. The dog is not a robot; they will have good and bad days. Dogs have emotions; they can be sad, happy, goofy, serious, chilled, or even irritated. Some may have "zoomies," and just need a good run in the yard to clear their head. Others may show signs of stress and anxiety and completely disengage from their handler. Handlers need to train to notice body language. Without a lot of experience, a handler may not notice their dog's behavior, especially when working. Learning body language and being your dog's best advocate–removing them from the situation if needed–is essential. This will allow your dog to continue to progress in training. Too much militant-type training, never taking a break, may cause delays and setbacks in training or could even cause the dog to "wash"--fail out of the service dog program.*

From Amanda: *Fear stages. I feel like most people don't recognize the fear stages as well as I try and explain it. Every time I explain it, I'm like, "Hey, your dog's in a fear stage; let's back off." They don't seem to see that, and they push through them too much. That's the biggest one.*

The other thing is, some people don't see that their dogs

need more of an outlet, and they need more than just service dog work; they need to have a sport on top of just being a service dog because their mentality is just a working dog. German shepherd people, mostly, are those types of handlers; their dogs need more, and they don't do enough. And then there are the people who do too much with their dogs and have these higher expectations when their dogs aren't meeting them, and I tell them to go back to basics and not move forward. They don't like me, at that point.

Other things I haven't seen in my dogs until my trainers told me about them are, again, Cor's lack of confidence in himself; how I was working Yaha too much and not letting him be a puppy; the unhealthy need in Yaha to be "doing something" every moment; Cor's adolescent boundary-pushing and the resulting need for me to be a bit firmer; Ozzy's hound-ness; Cor's fear stages; my letting Cor get away with training me and punkiness; and so, so many more.

This, if you remember, is one of the reasons that the one that would benefit from the service dog in training should not be the one to temperament test, even if they are a trainer, along with the reason the breeder shouldn't be the one to temperament test. We are very easily blinded to the annoyances or tics or shortcomings of those we love, which is unacceptable with a service dog. They need to be able to do their job, and if you are letting them run all over you, you are not loving them, or setting them up for success. Being permissive isn't the same as love. Especially in the situation where you're raising a living being to be a functional, decent member of society, which our dogs are, and have to be.

That said, sometimes the little quirks or goofinesses in our dogs are harmless and come from either their being a dog, or their breed. These differ from breed to breed, and dog to dog.

Question: What's special about this breed or your dog in particular that causes challenges sometimes?

The breed in general. Some people hate pits and have actively been aggressive towards us or caused us access issues and some people ADORE pits and have no respect for her, me, or our boundaries. --Kaleb Kelly

The breed is headstrong. I would not recommend ever trying to get a mix of these breeds. They are headstrong, but sensitive when you get angry at them. --River

She is STUBBORN! And hardheaded. She thinks she knows everything, and talks back. --Lauren Girsh

He's hard-headed and sensitive. --Rose family

He's so excited to work and please me that sometimes he just starts guessing instead of listening to what I'm asking for. He's also weird about the types of things he retrieves, like, with my other dogs, once they learned retrieval they'd pretty much pick up anything, even if it was new, but Sug doesn't like to pick up unfamiliar things without training it, which can be a problem if I need something that he hasn't worked with before. He also isn't a fan of loud noises so I have to be extra careful with that so it doesn't become a hindrance in his work. --Marleigh

She is so mouthy it's a little overbearing. She loves to nibble on my hands and feet, as well as chewing and ripping up toys and clothes of mine. --Sam

His nose! His nose always navigates to the floor. He loves to sniff the floor, so I have an actual command, "nose up," to tell him to stop sniffing the ground. --Janet

Incredibly intelligent, but sometimes hard to take care of physically due to grooming needs and my physical disabilities. --Leonard Duncan

Her hyperness. --Kelsey

He was too friendly with others and strangers sometimes. Had to train a lot of that out. --Anonymous

On the flip side of the same coin, however, some aspects and quirks differ from breed to breed and dog to dog that do the opposite, in that they help. Out of the gate, many of these can be seen as something that may cause challenges, when, in reality, if you work with them, they just add details and aspects of your relationship that you wouldn't get with other dogs.

Cor likes to jump up on people, and, when he doesn't add a shove at the end, I don't mind. We now have a command for it--hug.

As for his victory laps and jumping up on other people... still working on that, along with a handful of other puppy-isms.

What I'm trying to say, here, is that no dog is a robot. They all have quirks and mannerisms others won't. They won't understand what you want, all the time. But they have quirks and mannerisms others won't that will make your bond special and unique.

Question: What's special about this breed or your dog in particular that helps her/him do their job?

She is ALWAYS ready to go. --Kaleb Kelly

The breeds all together become either a very large dog like mine is, or a small lab like her sister did. --River

She has the endurance to go as much as I do; I'm always on the go with four active kids, work, and just life in general. --Lauren Girsh

He's big and thick. --Rose family

I still don't know a ton about poodles as a whole, since Sug is my first one, but I love that he has the energy to go all day with me, but can also chill all day if that's what I need. I love how much he loves to work and how happy he is all the time. He's also the first service dog I've had that is super cuddly and that's been good for me as well. --Marleigh

Clover is super empathetic and can tell when I'm about to have a mood change before I can myself. She licks at my face when I cry and cuddles next to me every night so I don't have nightmares. --Sam

Nothing special about his breed helps me aside from sniffing out his treats, giving me wet willies, or getting upset at the

squirrels on the roof. :) --Janet

Incredibly intelligent and eager to please, emotionally sensitive. --Leonard Duncan

Her knack to know what I need, even if it's to drive me crazy or her to act crazy at home; it's good because it distracts me and makes me calm down and smile. --Kelsey

He was small enough to sit in my lap in cars if needed, his coat was soft and smooth and not overly stimulating, and I needed a clingy boy. --Anonymous

Question: What do you consider unique to your dog/ training?

My living situation makes things unique--I'm pretty much constantly on the move as a college student with no home to go back to. This variety has helped JoJo during our training, but it's also been super stressful at times. --Leonard Duncan

How smart she is and how fast she learns things, and that if food is involved she will do anything. --Lauren Girsh

Our bond and our personalities. --Kelsey

Clover is the quirkiest animal I have ever come across. One moment she wants to nibble at my hands and feet all day, every day, and the next, she just wants to chill and nap right next to me. She is incredibly smart and sassy, and she knows it, too. Clover will give me this look that says, "I'm about to be naughty and do something bad," and then she will grab one of my stuffed animals or one of my shirts and run away with it. --Sam

He was a Cavalier King Charles Spaniel, much smaller than "traditional service dogs," but he was perfect for my needs. --Anonymous

Valor is mostly hound, so smelly treats are his absolute favorite, as much as I or anyone else may not like it. He is also a huge attention hog when it comes to his favorite people and will whine if other dogs are getting attention and not him. --Janet

I consider it unique that we train the way we need to. I

don't often stick to our program. Peach and I are in tune with our training and know what to do. --River

    Always trying something different. We've never had two days the same. --Kaleb Kelly

    Something that always really surprises people is that I had successfully trained three working service dogs completely on my own, but still chose to go with Scout's Legacy after that. The reason is that, because I was self-taught, I knew there were holes in my training so I wanted to learn from someone that had amazing, solid dogs with a philosophy I agreed with, and more experience than I had. --Marleigh

5. Mixed Advice

Question: Do you have any words of wisdom for those thinking of getting a dog that will require a bit of a heavier focus on grooming?

From FIGZ: *Our thought is you need to pick your battles. While poodles have hair that continually grows, it does not shed all over the house. So, in essence, you have controlled hair issues with non-shedding dogs. Because poodles grow hair so well, there are thousands of things you can try with them. Leave the hair long and fluffy, cut it short, try a mohawk or a goatee, or dye it the colors of the rainbow. Have fun with it!*

The hardest part of poodle hair is coat change. This is when the adult, more coarse and curly hair, starts coming in. Brushing every day, for about an hour on a standard poodle, is a necessity because the adult hair will wrap around the puppy hair and cause mats. Yes, they literally can mat while sleeping. Keeping the hair short, clean, and blow-dried during this time will help greatly. Coat change usually starts about the same time their hormones start to come in, around 9 months, and can continue till 12-18 months of age.

Since poodle hair is different from other dogs' fur, using a puppy or dog shampoo that is specially formulated for a poodle is best. Generic puppy and dog shampoo will strip the coat of the oil, make the hair brittle, cause more matting, and could make the hair break or fall out. If affordability is an issue, a higher quality, conditioning, anti-frizz human shampoo works well on a poodle. It is best to brush mats out when the hair is wet to avoid breakage. Use a detangler, spray and work into hair, brush out all the mats, then give a bath. If the dog is bathed with too many mats, the washing of the hair will make it worse. Drying the poodle's hair with a heavy-duty force dryer will straighten the hair leaving it fluffy and more manageable and causing the hair to mat less. The dryer can be used between baths to get out dirt and fluff the hair.

From Amanda: *I highly suggest investing in grooming supplies, because it's going to save you in the long run. Even if that means you're only getting one item at a time, it is still going to help save you a lot of time and effort as you go on. And if you know you're getting a heavy grooming dog, start investing before that dog gets there, because, man, as soon as that dog gets there, you are going to be spending a lot of money on that dog. And, you need to practice to get better. I know it's hard and it's one of those, "oh my goodness, there's a lot to learn," kind of things. The more you practice, the better it gets, though.*

With our heavy grooming dogs, you have to practice so your puppy understands what to expect when it comes to grooming. Your dogs are not born with this ability to be groomed by us, they have to be taught. So you have to teach your dog to sit still while being groomed, you have to teach them to handle the ear plucking, handle the nail trimming, handle the shaving, or any of the scissoring that needs to happen on this animal. All of it is a learned aspect, so making sure that you are teaching your puppy from a young age is important; your groomers can't do that. That is all up to the handler. Groomers can only see them once in a blue moon. It is up to the handlers to be able to put all that work into it so your dog is not stressed out while they are getting groomed. And, also, if you invest in the quality of grooming products such as a force dryer--not even just a blow dryer--get a nice force dryer, so that way you can fully groom them yourself. It'll save your wallet so much money because bath and blow dries alone are usually thirty-five bucks at groomers. Service dogs have to be clean. This is not an animal that is allowed to go out dirty, so it'll save you a lot of time and money by just doing it yourself.

Question: Is there anything I haven't asked about that you would like me to cover?

From Amanda: *So, something you didn't ask about that I'd like to discuss, I guess, is the fact that every disability is different. Just because someone with anxiety has a service dog and they're successful with it, does not mean that the next person with anxiety is going to be successful with a service dog. Every single person's disability is different, which means the way they handle their dog is going to be different.*

So, the idea and aspect that we need to be a mob mentality and to police the service dog community because they're not following these certain standards are turning into a bunch of bull-cocky and I'm over it. Every dog has to be worked according to their handler's needs, and just because it's not like yours does not mean it's incorrect.

The ADA is vague for a reason, and that is because it provided enough support there for our service dog handlers without restricting them. The more restrictions we start adding, the worse it's going to get for our service dog community, and, unfortunately, there are already things starting to come into place for more restrictions because of how many people are not following just the small standards we have for our dogs. And the small standards are potty trained, basic obedience trained, and socially able to handle the public access world. That's all they ask for--and task training, of course--but that's all they ask for. They don't ask for much. So, while, yes, with my company, I have a lot of expectations on my dogs, technically, most of our dogs that go to lesson four or five are service dogs in the ADA world.

Question: Is there anything I haven't asked about that you would like to share about this lifestyle?

People will stare and give you dirty looks. --Rose family
As much as I feel helped and saved by my service dog, I

have also had to cope with the crippling loneliness that has come from getting her. I have lost connections with a few close family members because of this change. I have been laughed at. I have been stared at. I have been flat-out told by kids younger than me that I don't need Clover, especially because she is a "vicious pit bull." It's gotten better over the seven months that I have had her, but it's still there in the back of my mind. Always. --Sam

Cherish them. --Anonymous

I truly wish more people in the general public were fully educated about service dogs. When I bring Valor to work, it's always like I'm bringing a giraffe instead. I'm always happy to answer questions; though, sometimes when I'm trying to work or just go about doing errands, it can be tiring. --Janet

It is hard, but don't give up if they are what you need. Even though my dog has some bad sides, the work she does for me is amazing. It won't be everything you expect. It will probably be nothing like that, for a lot, but the dog with you is so much more in life! They are amazing dogs who love you and care for you! They want to help. Don't give up. --River

Eventually, you become so attached to having your dog with you, that when you don't, you still find yourself saying "Let's go," "left/right," "stop," and people look at you weird. --Kaleb Kelly

Being a handler and trainer of service dogs has benefited so many people in my life besides me. All of my close friends and most of my family are educated on service dogs, now, and proper etiquette and are educating their children as well. Businesses see how Sugi acts and he serves as an example of how service dogs are supposed to behave. Even my dentist knows what behavior is acceptable and what her rights are, because of her relationship with me and all of my dogs. We have been able to help educate businesses, and even my university, of their rights to exclude out-of-control dogs, as well as the rights of the handlers. Being a trainer has also given me a sense of purpose and fulfillment that I thought was lost forever when my health declined and kept me from pursuing several of my passions. I know that even if I never accomplish anything else in my life, I've made a difference and done something amazing by being a service dog trainer. --Marleigh

If you're looking for a well-trained dog or an emotional support dog, ask trainers in your area if they have any dogs that didn't make it through their program. Nine times out of ten, the answer will be yes, and they will have made it far enough that basic obedience, and, quite likely, advanced obedience, will have been covered. If that falls through, look for RESPONSIBLE breeders that breed specifically for the service dog temperament and see if you can get on a waiting list for a puppy that doesn't pass the temperament test. They will have been raised as though they were going to be a service dogs for the first seven weeks before they were able to take the temperament test. (For a timeline reference: puppies can only leave Mama at or after eight weeks, although they should leave her as close to the eight-week mark as possible to bond with their new person at the natural time they're mentally ready for it.) After that, it'll be up to you to continue the training. Because--and this bit is for everyone: it doesn't matter how much or how good of training the puppy got before they started with you; if you don't keep it going, they'll lose it. It's like riding a bike or doing anything--use it or lose it.

6. Curtain!

I have alluded to it before, but, as tough as puppyhood is, and as much unsolicited attention that having a dog in a vest in public gets you, there is something no handler wants to think about--the dreaded monster that marks the end of the adventure: retirement.

No one can work forever. And being a service dog is no easy job, as I think I have pretty well described so far. But, we've all seen senior dogs, and I think we can all agree that they reach a point where asking them to turn lights on and off, pull wheelchairs, put themselves under a convulsing someone, and be on constant alert to notice the next warning of their human's monster rearing its ugly head in time to warn them, becomes inhumane.

A service dog's working life is, on average, six to eight years. Training takes about two years. That means, however long the dog lives, they retire around eight to ten years old. There's still quite a bit of time left in a dog's life at that point, though. What this means, is that, when they retire, you have to decide if you keep the dog as a pet, or give them up to live as a pet in someone else's home.

While I've never dealt with a dog at this time of life, I refer you back to when Yaha washed as at least a taste of the situation.

I want to be able to keep Cor once he retires, but I was unable to do so when Yaha washed. There were a couple of reasons beyond what we've already covered.

For one, one of the reasons Yaha washed was that he became possessive to the point of danger. So bringing another dog into the house to, essentially, take over his job, wouldn't have sat well with him.

For another, I wasn't able to keep up with his energy, especially when he wasn't burning it with outings. I was already struggling to get work in, forget about any downtime.

And then there was my budget. As we've already covered, a service dog is not an inexpensive commitment, and my budget was starting to feel it with buying so many packs of antlers and treats, and food every month. If I was going to bring another dog in... well, it wouldn't have been wise. And, you don't want to run out of finances part way into this and have to drop out of the program and training because you can't pay for the dog anymore.

In the case of an older, retiring dog, there are also the factors of where the dogs will be while you're at work or school. The end result of service dog training is that the dog ends up going everywhere with you. Once they retire, however, they don't have the same special allowances as they did while they were working.

As a dog gets older, too... well, vet expenses tend to go up. And, when bringing a puppy into your home, there's about a six-month span where the vet expenses are *quite* hefty.

Don't get me wrong--I've begun to think about these necessities at Cor's age because I want to be able to keep him when we get there.

As always, defer to your trainer's advice for how to handle any new (or not new) situation, as they've been doing this for notably longer than either you or me. They also know your dog. They know you. They can see things you can't (like if a dog isn't going to be a good fit, for example). Even when it hurts, listen to them.

If it's best to let the dog live with another family, let me assure you of a few things I was worried about--even if I wouldn't let myself admit that I was.

1. Neither you nor your trainer wants your dog to go to a bad home. If you let your trainer help you here and are picky about who they go to,* you will find a place.

*As I've mentioned before, if you get your dog from a responsible breeder, they make it a condition that, should you ever be unable to keep the dog, for whatever reason, it goes back to them. If you did get your puppy from a breeder, have a three-way discussion with you, your trainer, and the puppy's breeder in this situation.

2. Just because the dog no longer lives with you does not mean they will forget you. The first time we visited Yaha at his new home,* it took him a couple of seconds, but there was a clear moment he remembered my scent, and placed it. He would go back and forth between me and his new people the entire time, very aware of who I was, and what was going on. When we were leaving, he tried to get in our van, but once he understood he was staying, there was no consternation or conflict on his face.

When I dogsit for him, he has no hesitation about crawling up in my lap as he does with his people (and never used to do with me), trying to fool me into thinking he can be a lap dog (he's now, like, eighty pounds to my hundred thirty), and falling asleep.

*Don't visit too close to the time they left. Let them get used to their new people--give them a chance to, and don't expect failure. This is just as much of a difficult time--and a new situation--for them as it is for you. Possibly more, because you knew this was coming. It takes about three days for a dog to get the feel for a new place, three weeks for them to get comfortable with a new routine, and about three months for them to accept any new people as "their people." Give them time to settle in with the new people. But feel free to ask for pictures and updates. If you are anything like me, they will do your heart good.

3. They have not forgotten their training. When I visited that first time, we stayed for dinner. With no prompting, Yaha lay at my feet just like he used to.

4. Their new people love them just as much as you still will, even if it's not the same way.

It's not the same as the transition of service dog to pet. It's still not easy or the same, though. Their girls have (somehow) gotten him to tolerate doggy Christmas pajamas; someone would've died had we tried that, I am ninety-nine percent certain.

While he did not like the pool of a friend of mine, he will now jump into theirs and play whenever he can get away with it, and, sometimes, even when he can't. He wakes his girls up with kisses in the morning. They find humor in the combination of a lab's jaws and a German shepherd's bite which means no toy they've yet found can hold up to his love. They are a far more exercise-centric family than I could ever be, taking him for several-mile walks in the mornings, and letting him romp around off leash for far farther than I could ever trust him to be because he will come back when his man calls his name.

It's not the way I loved him, because it's the life I couldn't give him.

You will give your dog a life no one else could, and whoever gets them in retirement will give them a life you can't, but that doesn't mean you can't be a part of it.

Friend, listen to me. If you choose this path, you are signing on to have your heart torn numerous times, and torn out at one point, for sure. But I can guarantee you will never have anything else love you as this dog will. It's up to you to choose if that's worth the pain of repeating every decade or so. If you keep them after retirement, you just put the pain off. If you give them up during retirement, you won't be the one to see their last breath. That's also something you need to consider in choosing what happens after retirement. Which pain can you take? Can you take either or only one?

Friend, this is not an easy road.

But, if you were to ask me, I'd have to tell you that, for the unconditional love and added freedom this dog will give you, all the nips and bites and embarrassment and attention and pain are worth it.

But you have to choose for yourself.

And, barring unforeseen consequences, you will see them as both an ears-too-big-for-their-body puppy, and you will survive them. Can you take that? Be honest with yourself, friend, because if you can't, you can't worm your way out of the pain once you've fallen in love with them. Be honest with yourself now, friend, I'm begging you. Because, after you say yes to their big, soulful eyes... I'm not going to say you're trapped, but you're trapped.

Question: If you could tell someone going into this anything about retirement, what would it be?

From Amanda: *Retirement is going to happen in a dog's career. Every dog retires just like every person retires. A service dog will retire in their own time frame. Honestly, I've seen dogs retire as early as five years of age, and then as late as fourteen. I've seen it all. And, so, I always tell people you have to go off of the dog itself: their health, their mentality, and work from there. You have to be prepared that retirement could come early, or it could come later. I have had dogs retire at an older age, and I have had dogs retire from one day working great, to the next day not being able to work at all. So retirement is a very hard subject for a lot of people just because nobody wants to lose their service dog.*

Once you get to the point of comfort with your animal, it is like you don't even have to think about breathing. When you're breathing, it's a natural response. Honestly, working with a fully trained and bonded team is very similar to that; you don't have to think about it, you just get out there, you live your life, and it's so nice and so easy. When you have to get back into training again, that is like a kink in your plans, so people who have had a service dog and then have to get a new one... usually that second dog is harder to live with for them than the first one. And then, usually by the third dog, they realize that it's going to be difficult, and the third service dog is easier than the first two, and it's kind of a funny transition.

Signs to look for when you're looking at a dog for retirement are going to be things such as: not willing to work, starting to ignore commands, and health signs. You have to watch for their movement; a lot of dog world people and service dog people do not understand how to watch a dog's movement, and I wish more people would, because, if you don't know that your dog is walking weirdly and get it to the vet to get it checked out--if you help them push through that pain--then you could be retiring that dog sooner than you thought. Your dog's health is everything when it comes to retirement. If they are not healthy, they should not be working. So, keeping them in tip-top shape is very, very important.

Other important things are the behavioral aspects. If your dog suddenly cannot handle working in public anymore, the dog needs to retire. And it's hard, but it's going to have to happen for their safety and yours.

This life is hard, friend. This has been repeated several times throughout this book because it's true.

I beg you to consider all this before committing one way or another.

Either way, though?

Take courage, friend. You were not born to fail. You will find your path. I believe that with all my heart. I truly do.

I can't wait to hear your story!

Acknowledgments

I can't say I know how to write these, but after trawling through many books' acknowledgments, it seems I just list who I am thankful for in this process. This is yet another problem--I've got far too many people I get to thank to think that I won't forget someone and end up with a whole other chapter back here. But, I can't simply go without, as I can't thank these people enough, and can only hope to give some semblance of the enormity of my gratitude. So, begging your pardon for anyone I miss (that will likely be added in later versions), here we go.

First, most and always, to my Lord and God--for life, for breath, for my seizures, my dogs, family, and friends, and, of course, this life that is never boring. You've brought me further than I could've ever dared to dream. Thanks, Dad.

Thank you to my mum, dad, and sisters--Marina and Josie--for watching Cor at this time when I'm in Wisconsin. Thank you Dad and Josie in particular for keeping up on Cor's walks and energy-burning so that he isn't bouncing off the walls, driving everyone crazy. Y'all are extraordinary sitters and walkers. Anyone would be lucky to have y'all as a rope team.

To Amanda of Scout's Legacy, and Kerry and Tanya of FIGZ Poodles for their immense and intimate knowledge of this world that I couldn't hope to have after merely two years of dog training under tutelage. To them, too, for all the questions I've asked and concerns I've presented that didn't make it in the book. I cannot express the enormity of the debt of gratitude I owe them for calming me down again when I come to any and all of them worried, panicked, or just unsure. I wouldn't have made it this far without them, and for that, I can never repay them in full.

To all those who answered question after question that I spat out with no clue where they'd end up. To the handlers: Kaleb

Kelly, River, Ivy Hotz, Lauren Girsh, Rose Family, Marleigh, Sam, Janet, Leonard Duncan, and Kelsey. To the families of Scooby Doo's handler, and Peach's handler.

To my mum. Thank you for your knowledge and wisdom in the world of getting books from a loose idea to a physical product that I can hold. Thank you for showing me that the mountain is just a hill and that it is more than surmountable.

To the creators of 4thewords. Thank you for making getting the words on paper fun, and for making a blank page so much less daunting.

To all those who've answered my questions about various aspects of writing and ISBNs and book covers and marketing on the various forums and discussion boards I haunt. It truly is easier to walk a path already made, and your footprints on the path are invaluable.

To the lovely folks at GetCovers for this wonderful cover. I still can't believe my name is on a book; thank y'all for making it such a lovely one!

To the folks with NaNoWriMo. Thanks for training me to write each day, and to view 50,000 words as a relatively simple endeavor.

To all my writer friends. Thank you for making discussions about writing, books, and theories commonplace, and cultivating my love for making my own. I want signed copies of all y'all's books!

To all those teachers who've always believed in me and pushed me to be more than I thought I could be. Mrs. Giesler, Miss Mary, Mrs. Staudinger, to you in particular. Thank you for some of the best times and great years!

To my friend Amara, who buried spurs in my sides when she began writing, thanks to my (sometimes unhealthy) competitive spirit.

To all those who read my rantings about this life on fieldsoffavor.us, and especially to all those who comment and send me messages after reading my posts. Thank you for giving me a place and an audience to play with words and the thoughts and feelings this life brings up. Thank you for allowing me to be the conduit with which you hear the magic words: "This is normal," You were not born to fail. <3

I wouldn't be here without any of you. I cannot thank any of you enough. Know that I love you all, and am cheering for you and your dreams just as you encouraged mine, whether you knew what they were or not, and regardless of whether we're still in touch. I love you all.

About The Author

Lauryn Walton is a young woman born in Wisconsin and currently splitting her time between housesitting in Texas and helping homeschool her cousin in Wisconsin. If you find her, you will almost always find her fluffy service sidekick--who may believe she is around to simply cater to his desires for snuggles and play when he isn't her additional 4 feet to independence.

Lauryn has been drowning in words since before she was born and is happy to stay that way. She runs the website fieldsoffavor.us and its subdomains, where she shares her adventures and some tips and insights into the service dog life for those investigating this world. To learn more about what it's like to be a service dog handler, or get some help transitioning into the lifestyle, click on over and drop her a line or sign up for the email list! On her little slice of the abyss that is the internet you will find the stories she so avidly writes, (many more books coming soon,) as well as her crocheted handiwork.